MAKE MONEY ON YOUTUBE

START AND MONETIZE A NEW YOUTUBE CHANNEL IN 6 SIMPLE STEPS

GINA HORKEY

LUKE ATKINSON

Copyright © 2020 by Gina Horkey

All rights reserved. No part of this publication may be reproduced, distributed, or transmitted in any form or by any means, including photocopying, recording, or other electronic or mechanical methods, without the prior written permission of the publisher, except in the case of brief quotations embodied in reviews and certain other non-commercial uses permitted by copyright law.

The information provided within this book is for general informational purposes only. While the authors try to keep the information up-to-date and correct, there are no representations or warranties, express or implied, about the completeness, accuracy, reliability, suitability or availability with respect to the information, products, services, or related graphics contained in this book for any purpose. Any use of this information is at your own risk.

Any advice that is provided in this book is based on the experience of the authors and does not reflect the opinion of the distributor. All opinions expressed in this book are solely the opinion of the authors.

Disclaimer:
Some of the links in this book may be affiliate links. If you click them and decide to buy something, we may be paid a commission. This won't cost you any extra. We only include links to products or services that we either use or would happily use ourselves.

CONTENTS

Free Bonus	iv
1. Introduction	1
2. Move Past the Fear	10
3. How To Make Money On YouTube	20
4. Create Your YouTube Plan (Step One)	29
5. Set up Your YouTube Account (Step Two)	41
6. Record Your First Three Videos (Step Three)	47
7. Launch Your Channel (Step Four)	63
8. Gain Your First 100 Subscribers (Step Five)	72
9. Monetize Your Channel (Step Six)	80
10. Offer YouTube Marketing Services	93
11. YouTube Success	102
12. Conclusion	112
Notes	114
About Gina Horkey	115
About Lucas Atkinson	116
Excerpt: Make Money As A Podcast Producer	117

FREE BONUS

As a thank-you for buying our book, we have created some bonus resources to help you on your journey. These resources will help you:

> Master the skills you'll need to start and monetize your YouTube channel

> Learn to make must-see videos using simple steps

> Create a flexible work schedule while providing a sustainable income

Download your bonus resources at:
uploaduniversity.com/book-bonus/

1

INTRODUCTION

Have you fantasized about becoming the next YouTube star, or about starting a freelance gig that feeds your passion and your bank account? Perhaps you're already enjoying the freelance life, unencumbered by the nine-to-five grind and a boss looking over your shoulder, and are looking for a new income source?

As a self-employed individual, your income — and your limits — are boundless. And within all the possibilities of making a living online, you're here because you're curious about what YouTube has to offer you.

Here's our answer: money and free marketing.

You can make money on YouTube by monetizing your own channel, driving traffic to your existing blog, or by becoming a YouTube Marketing Specialist.

We're here to show you how to harness the power of YouTube as a free marketing tool for your business, your client's business, or your individual brand. These are just a few of the ways that you can profit from YouTube and escape the corporate rut.

This book is for you if you're looking to:

1. Grow a new or existing business with the help of YouTube.

2. Help other business owners harness the power of video marketing.

3. Become "internet famous" by starting and monetizing your own channel.

You may be wondering, *There are already so many channels on YouTube. Would anyone even watch my videos?*

The answer to this question is an overwhelming yes!

YouTube is the most popular video hosting platform and the second largest search engine in the world, outranked only by its parent company, Google.

Over 1 billion people use YouTube, and it's still growing. More than 300 hours of video are uploaded to YouTube every minute, with almost 5 billion video views every day. The number of hours people have spent watching videos on YouTube (also known as "watch time") was up 60% in 2020, the fastest growth since 2018.

These numbers show how much potential there is on YouTube. Of the 1 billion people watching YouTube videos, a fraction of them — even if it's only 100 or 1,000 people — could be your viewers. The time to get involved is now.

In this book we teach you how to start and grow a profitable YouTube channel. You don't need experience, an existing channel, or even an established business. We guide you step-by-step, from your first subscriber to your next 100, and beyond.

For virtual service providers, specializing in YouTube marketing is a gold mine of opportunity. We show you what skills you can offer clients, how to manage their channels, and how to market their businesses more effectively.

Figuring everything out on your own is daunting and inefficient. It can quickly lead to burnout. We've been down this path before, and we've mastered YouTube (by making the mistakes) along the way. We urge you to learn from our successes and failures, avoid the common has given him the freedom to control his schedule and be available for his daughter whenever he is needed.

In 2018 Lucas took his business to the next level by launching his first YouTube channel. He monetized his channel within nine months. With a thriving channel and numerous personal and professional connections formed from YouTube, Lucas understands the immense potential of this social media platform.

After Lucas consulted on Horkey HandBook's YouTube presence and helped optimize their channel, the pair realized they had something special to offer the community. Gina and Lucas saw the opportunity to teach virtual service providers how to help business owners incorporate video into their marketing strategy. They realized that together they could show the community just how much YouTube can offer to everyone.

Read, Then Do

While the opportunity is there, sifting through all the unknowns of YouTube and freelancing can be daunting. Making the leap from full-time employee to business owner takes guts. But as scary as this moment is, it is also exhilarating.

As you move into video marketing, there's a near-infinite number of niches and possibilities for you. And as you weed through them, some will "fit" you better than others.

Some days are exciting and energizing. Other days leave you in confusion or exhaustion — and that's okay. Rome wasn't built in a day. We're here to guide you through the process.

The good news is that the mistakes you make in the infancy of your channel are fixable. You can always delete and start fresh, homing in on the topics you'd rather cover. But what you can't fix later is how much time you spend on your channel. We can help you avoid the common pitfalls and fast-track your success. However, it's essential that you commit to doing the work (more on this later).

pitfalls, and bring your wildest dreams into a successful Y(
reality.

But first... you're probably curious to know who "we" are.

Meet the Fearless Sibling Duo

We're a brother-and-sister team. Gina is the founder of Horke
Book.com, where she's been teaching people how to offer virtu
lancing services since 2014. Since then, she's coached nearly
students.

Gina keeps a pulse on the current marketplace, the most
marketing strategies, and exactly what business owners ne
with. She understands the importance of video marketi
actively applies it to reach Horkey HandBook's target audier
teaches her students how to stand out from the crowd usin
pitching techniques and knows exactly what it takes to
online.

When Gina started her own freelance writing side hustle
spring of 2014, she had no idea that Horkey HandBook would
become a leading resource for virtual assistants and freelance
She also didn't anticipate joining forces with her family, but
other plans. Each member of her immediate family has
alongside her at some point, and the latest addition is her
Lucas Atkinson.

Meanwhile, Lucas is an entrepreneur with several bu
under his belt. He walked away from a 20-year career
annual salary of over $100k to work from home, and most
tantly, for himself. After starting off in commercial const
the pull of being his own boss was too tempting. The bul
work became running e-commerce websites with su
brands.

One reason Lucas started his entrepreneur journey was his d
who was diagnosed with epilepsy as a toddler. Being self-er

This book lays out all the information you need to master YouTube. But simply reading this book isn't enough. You need to act on what you learn.

In the rest of this chapter, we show you how to get the most from this book. The process is simple, but each step is equally important. Let's take a look.

Download the Companion Resources

There are a lot of moving parts when setting up and growing a YouTube channel. We've seen people start a channel, hit a setback, get frustrated, and give up. Usually it's because they've missed some crucial points about how to optimize their channel for success. We don't want you to do the same.

To keep you on track, we've created downloadable resources that accompany this book. These checklists and worksheets provide key points to review, as well as a guide for implementing what you learn.

The worksheets are a helpful review of the entire book, all in one place, and will ensure you follow all the action steps to have your channel up and running in the shortest time possible.

You can download the companion resources at: **uploaduniversity.com/book-bonus/**

Schedule Time To Do the Work

We've set out all the materials for you. The learning part should come easily. Now all you need to do is set aside time to work through this book.

Come up with a schedule and make sure it's realistic. It's more valuable to give yourself two hours every week than going all-in for one week and burning out early.

Do what you must to make space in your calendar. This might mean asking your partner to help with meal prep so that you can focus on your channel for an extra hour or paying a babysitter for an hour or two each week. You may need to get up earlier or work late at night. Find what works for you.

Treat your passion with the respect it deserves. Set aside a regular time to read, then implement the action steps. Once you commit to the process, your goals will come that much closer to reality.

Commit To Finishing

And on the topic of commitment, set an intention to finish the entire book. After all, this is not just a book. It's a valuable resource packed with insider information.

There are six steps to making money on YouTube. And you must complete all of them... in the correct order. The six steps are:

1. Create Your YouTube Plan

2. Set Up Your YouTube Account

3. Record Your First Three Videos

4. Launch Your Channel

5. Gain Your First 100 Subscribers

6. Monetize Your Channel

We know it's tempting to jump around, and even to read multiple chapters at once. However, we've laid out the material in this order — and with these specific action steps — for a reason. Trust the process and follow through.

A successful entrepreneur makes learning a lifelong goal. But don't get stuck in the learning loop. This is where you take in so much information that you don't know where to begin. It's common to feel this paralysis when you start a new business.

So commit to moving through the book at a regular pace and completing the steps in order. You can do this! We promise.

Practice These Four Success Principles

We know that starting any new venture can be challenging. And so we've also compiled four best practices to help you stay on track. Practice each of these success principles, and you will achieve your goals.

1. Take It Seriously

If you want to succeed on YouTube, you must take it seriously. Treat it like a business. Show up and do the work each day, even when you don't feel like it. Just as you would for an employer.

Let's set our expectations right. Building a channel from scratch doesn't pay right away. It might feel like these hours aren't giving you the best return, because the money will come later.

But if you follow the steps outlined in this book, you'll be well on your way toward your goal, whether it's monetization or getting the most out of YouTube via marketing.

2. Develop Your Content

If you're creating your own channel, you've probably already thought about the type of content you want to produce. Follow your wildest dreams here (within reason)! Choose something you care about.

If you're passionate about your topic, then you will still have something to say, nine or 20 or 35 videos down the line.

Later in this book, we cover every aspect of developing content in detail.

3. Be Consistent

We cannot stress enough how important it is to have a plan. Your plan is a schedule that forces you to post regular content. Why should you care about this? Because your consistency will build your audience.

Once you start on a schedule, stick to it. You can end up publishing more frequently, but you don't want to upload less often. And while we're on this topic... you must be consistent with live streaming, too. Don't be deterred if you only have a few people watching at first. Just keep showing up. We talk more about YouTube Live in later chapters.

I (Lucas) did not jump into YouTube Live straight away. It can take a while to feel comfortable broadcasting to a live audience. But stay with it, and you will see the benefits. Initially, I uploaded one video every two weeks and went live on Sunday afternoons. Then, when I could manage more, I added a second live video on Wednesday evenings.

4. Keep Improving Your Channel

Just as you treat your YouTube channel like a business, view the face of your channel as your website homepage. Continue adding to your channel and keep everything up-to-date. If you maintain a professional appearance, your YouTube channel will be like your LinkedIn page on steroids.

As you learn more about the elements of a successful YouTube channel, you can improve your design and enhance your video content with video intros and outros. Over time, you will evolve and enhance your brand in all areas of your business. As you do this, focus on reflecting and furthering your brand through your YouTube channel.

Join the YouTube Community

Joining YouTube is not like creating a profile on another social media site. Depending on your current career, you may not be in the habit of speaking to anyone, let alone hundreds or thousands of fans. And yet YouTube can be an incredibly warm and supportive place.

I (Lucas) have made enduring friendships on YouTube, and many have become professional connections. It's one benefit of having a social media space that also makes money. Your friends are your connections.

When I was at the beginning of my YouTube journey and had just over 100 subscribers, a fan emailed me through my About page. This guy was a YouTuber in my niche, and he invited me to another (larger) YouTuber's live stream.

He knew that connecting with this other channel could be important for me. I attended the live stream and in the following week I gained 50 new subscribers. This affirms a basic principle about YouTube: people want to connect and support each other.

However, you get out of it as much as you put in. Show up for your favorite channels, and they'll show up for you.

There's a mutual social investment in helping one another out on YouTube. Not that it feels like an obligation — it doesn't! You can like and support the channels you genuinely enjoy. Connect with people you admire and those that inspire you.

We promise that there will be channels (and supportive fans as well as new friends) who will have your back.

Make Your Passion a Career on YouTube

You've come this far. You are already paving a path towards YouTube success. Now keep it coming.

We want you to be successful with the resources we're giving you. Commit to the action steps and worksheets. Actually do them! They are pointing you in the right direction at the end of every chapter.

If you read and follow the action steps in order, we promise that even if you're a beginner, you'll build a profitable YouTube channel.

In this book we cover everything you need to set up, optimize, and monetize your YouTube channel, and/or market your YouTube skills to clients. Depending on how much time you give, you can lay the foundation for your YouTube career in 30 days or less.

Are you in? Let's get started.

2

MOVE PAST THE FEAR

Before we start planning your YouTube career, we need to discuss fear. Many new entrepreneurs fail to reach their goals because they do not take the time to address their innermost thoughts and feelings.

We have seen thousands of excited newbies fall at the first — or tenth — hurdle. And there *will* be obstacles for you to overcome. Let's make sure you're ready for them.

There are a hundred reasons why starting something new might spark fear. Maybe no one among your family or close friends works from home, let alone online. We've all been in that place where we receive well-intentioned but judgmental questions.

Ten (or even five) years ago, most people hadn't heard of the term "online influencer." Today, though, this is a viable career choice that many people are making. There is so much opportunity on YouTube and the sooner you start, the sooner you can take advantage of all it has to offer.

Here are some doubts that you — or the people around you — may have about starting an online business:

An online income won't be enough to support my family.

How am I going to make it? There are already many YouTube channels out there.

Starting a business takes more time than I have.

I don't have enough experience.

I want to make it on YouTube, but I don't know where to start.

I'm too shy. I can't imagine putting my face on the internet.

We've also faced these doubts and questions — believe us! We're only human, after all.

But here are the facts: hard work and persistence can raise a freelance (or influencer) income above that of corporate America, and following your passion has a deeply satisfying psychological result. In other words, chasing your dreams is good for you.

However, even if you get past the social pressure to stick with a nine-to-five, you may still have doubts about how to run your business. This is normal. The fear doesn't go away after week one or two of creating your business.

Starting something new requires putting yourself out there, exposing yourself to criticism and rejection. It's only human to want to avoid such an outcome. That's why you must change your mindset around fear.

How you think determines how you face the inevitable ups and downs in your business. It influences how you handle mistakes and failures, because problems happen, and you need to know that you can bounce back. In fact, with the right mindset you can learn and grow from each setback. This is what ultimately leads to your success.

When you embrace the unknown — and face your most intimidating fears — you can work through what's holding you back. Being able to confront fear head-on is how you move from self-doubt to exhilaration and courageously create the life you want.

In the rest of this chapter, we explore the most common obstacles that stand between you and your dreams and how to work through them.

Fear #1: I Don't Have Enough Time

I (Gina) know how hectic life can be, both at work and at home. But I want to offer you some tips. Truth be told, you don't need to set aside a lot of extra time to start your side hustle.

How? The secret is to plan for your time; otherwise, you'll watch it slip away.

Back in 2014, I started to consider launching my own business offering freelance writing services online. At the time, I was working at a financial firm. While it was great to have a stable job, I was itching to make a career shift and be my own boss.

But at that time, my life was crazy. We had a toddler and a 10-month-old that I was still nursing. And as the breadwinner for our household, I couldn't quit my job to launch a business. I needed to be sure that my new business could match my corporate salary.

The only solution was to work my side hustle as well as my day job. This meant applying time management to the max!

While attempting this challenging schedule, I picked up the following time management tips. Just six months after starting, I was earning over $4,000 per month. Two months later, I quit my day job.

1. Schedule Time in Your Calendar

In the previous chapter, we asked you to look at your calendar and consider your responsibilities. Find an hour or two every day that you can set aside for your YouTube channel or YouTube marketing business.

I jump-started my side career by waking up at 4:30 a.m. every morning. That meant I could work for an hour or two before I had to nurse the baby, take a shower, and get ready to head to work.

You may be thinking that 4:30 a.m. sounds like crazy talk. But honestly, the early morning is what worked for me. Find a time that you can commit to as well. Perhaps you're a night owl or can squeeze in an hour during your lunch break.

And remember — these hours are for business-building activities only. Protect your time and hold yourself accountable. Always work on your business when you said you would.

2. Be Consistent

Maybe you can only commit to 30 minutes per day in the beginning. Or perhaps you can manage two hours on the weekends. That's fine. A focused 30 minutes is productivity gold, especially when you can keep the momentum up throughout the week.

All you need to do is use your time wisely. And you know what? You might even discover that you can get more done in less time when you plan and prioritize.

Which brings us to tip number three...

3. Prioritize Tasks

Be smart with the time you have. What can you do now that will make the biggest impact on your business?

Throughout this book we provide checklists and steps to keep you on track, especially at the beginning, when those first hours are wide open.

As a new freelancer or influencer, it's easy to get lost in the weeds, spending time on unnecessary details. You must avoid doing that. Always do the essential tasks first.

After I landed my first freelancing client, I dedicated my first hours each day making good on my assignments. I spent any extra time applying for more gigs. I continued with that pattern until I took on as many clients as I could.

Eight months later, I walked away from my corporate job and didn't look back.

Fear # 2: Only Viral Videos Make Real Money

This fear might be the reason you opened this book. You are probably wondering:

Can I make money on YouTube? Or, can I make a decent living doing YouTube marketing for clients?

Let's start with the first question. It's easy to focus on the biggest channels or the most popular videos when we think about "making it" on YouTube.

A lot of people get into YouTube with the goal of going viral. And if you achieve 1-5 million views on a video, then you can indeed make a big pile of cash. The money — and the fame — can be appealing.

But here's the deal: YouTube doesn't only pay the channels that have millions or tens of millions of views. You can also make money with videos that aren't meant to be "viral."

We're not here to give you advice on how to spike your popularity into the millions. That's not what we're about. We're here to support your business and help it grow at a predictable pace. Growing your channel steadily can be profitable and is much easier to sustain over the long term.

We discuss all the opportunities to make money on YouTube — without going viral — in Chapter Three. For now here's a peek into how much ad revenue you can expect after you monetize your channel.

YouTube channels receive $18 per 1,000 ad views, or $3-$5 for 1,000 video views.

But these numbers may seem abstract. Let's take a closer look at how these figures can make an income for any channel and in any niche.

It's common to see channels with only 8k-10k subscribers earning $50 per day in ad revenue alone. If we scale that $50 a day to a whole year, that's $18,250 in ad revenue. And that's excluding any growth from consistently uploading new content.

These channels are not huge and are definitely not in the "viral" category. But they can make some serious side hustle income on YouTube. Adding $18,250 per year is nothing to sneeze at, especially for a passive income stream. With YouTube videos, the money keeps coming in once the initial work of uploading them has been completed.

After you monetize your YouTube channel, passive income grows from ad revenue on your videos. You continually drive income back to your brand (and bank account). And you gain the freedom to work on other aspects of your personal and professional life.

But there's more. Ad revenue is not the only way to make money on YouTube.

When it comes to calculating your total income from YouTube, there are multiple factors at play. There's passive income on older videos, ad revenue from new videos, as well as YouTube channel memberships and YouTube Super Chat.

In channel memberships, subscribers pay a fee to access the content on your channel. Super Chat is an option to monetize your channel when you go live. When a viewer goes to a live stream, they see a dollar bill symbol in the chat screen. If they click on this symbol, they can send you a dollar amount.

And while we're talking about what makes YouTube worthwhile, we can't leave out video marketing. Businesses are taking advantage of YouTube to reach new audiences hungry for video content. A business may have a small- or medium-sized YouTube channel that they never intend to monetize directly on YouTube. The marketing power of YouTube in and of itself is attractive enough.

And we haven't even touched on the value that making new connections can add to your business.

As we move forward, we'll help you decide how you want to use YouTube. Your goal may not be monetization, and that's okay. There's so much else to get out of YouTube. We'll help you make the most of it either way.

Fear #3: I'm Too Shy To Appear on Camera

For some people, the idea of talking in front of a camera makes every muscle in their body tense up. Some even break out in a cold sweat. We have been there. But we promise that the first video is the most difficult. After that, they get easier.

If you're already thinking, *No way, I'm not showing my face on the internet*, then, good news— you don't have to!

Face-to-camera videos are not your only option. There are many kinds of YouTube videos, including those that involve a voice-over, or music, with different visuals. As you brainstorm your niche, keep this in mind. We talk more about finding your niche in Chapter Four.

But let's back up to the "camera shy" folks, because we don't want you to choose your niche primarily based on fear. Let's say you're committed to the talking-head format. We have some tips to calm your nerves for those first few videos.

1. Clean up.

When you look good, you feel good. Put on a clean shirt and comb your hair. Take some time to create the best version of yourself. Although there's no such thing as a professional dress code on YouTube, you can still look great.

Knowing that you're presenting your best self helps you feel confident. And it doesn't hurt to keep the area where you're about to record clean and tidy. We're not talking a deep clean. But consider what impression you want to show your viewers.

2. Make a pre-shoot ritual.

Before shooting your first video, take some time to get into the right mindset. We're talking relaxed (but not too relaxed) and confident.

Make a cup of tea and hold your favorite mug. Or take a 10-minute stretch and do some push-ups. Say a positive affirmation or meditate to quiet your mind and calm your nerves.

Do whatever works for you. Shake out the nerves and pump yourself up. Tell yourself, *I got this!*

3. Let go of your inner perfectionist.

If you're new to recording yourself, you might be surprised (or horrified) by watching your own videos. You also might stumble on your words, and that's okay. Let the camera roll and keep going. Restarting the video over and over again increases your nerves.

Try not to get frustrated with yourself. Give yourself some silent encouragement (*You got this! It's going to be okay!*) and don't forget to breathe.

Rather than aiming to get every word right the first time, just record something. Done is better than perfect. Most likely, it will display you as a real person who talks naturally and looks great.

Sometimes it's best to wait until the next day to watch the video back. When you approach things from a less judgmental frame of mind, you'll see you were better than you thought.

Finally, don't overthink it. We know of many shy people who have conquered their fear of being on camera. Sure, there may always be butterflies in your stomach while you're recording. But that fluttery feeling — it's a bit like excitement, right? That's because nerves and excitement elicit the same physiological response in your body.

And if you're excited about making videos, then you must care about what you're doing. This is the kind of work you're meant to do. So don't let that fear stop you.

Fear #4: I Have No Experience

Many newbies lack confidence in their skills. They doubt whether they can be successful, or if they can do what a client needs, or if they're even qualified to have their own business.

These feelings are normal, especially at the beginning. I (Lucas) had no idea where to start creating my YouTube channel. I jumped right in and taught myself everything I could, learning as I went.

We know that learning new things is hard. Fresh beginnings are difficult for everyone, whether you're faced with lack of time, lack of confidence, or lack of experience.

There's a learning curve for any new skill and any significant career move. If you want to make money on YouTube, you must set yourself up to be a lifelong learner because the technology keeps changing. YouTube itself frequently changes its guidelines. And while it isn't difficult to keep up, you must adapt to new rules and regulations.

Outside of that, successful entrepreneurs commit to continually learning. It's through learning and growth that you reach your potential. As a freelancer, having specialized skills means you can charge higher rates. And as an entrepreneur, the faster you overcome obstacles, the more easily you reach your goals.

So set yourself up for long-term success from the start. Give yourself extra days to learn and push yourself past the bounds of your current skill set.

Action Steps

1. Write down the reason(s) why you want to explore a career on YouTube.

2. Now identify the top fear holding you back from realizing your

potential on YouTube. Write an action plan to overcome it with three realistic action items.

* * *

In Chapter Three we explore further the different methods you can make money on YouTube so that you can decide what kind of YouTube career you want, then start planning a new future for yourself.

3

HOW TO MAKE MONEY ON YOUTUBE

In the previous chapter, we summarized some of the ways you can make money on YouTube. In this chapter we dig deeper and explore the full potential of this powerful platform.

You (or your client) may already have a YouTube channel. After all, YouTube is a perfect platform to advertise a business online. Even a few short videos can engage potential customers. But are you aware of *all* the methods a channel can bring new cash into a business?

When you harness the power of YouTube, you:

1. Improve Google search rankings and reach new customers or clients.

2. Bring in additional cash streams, including passive income.

Let's examine each of these opportunities in turn.

Improve Search Ranking and Reach New Clients

Most businesses know how important it is for customers to find them via a Google search. This is why they pour money into SEO (search engine optimization) and SEM (search engine marketing) services.

They want their content to appear on the first page of Google when someone is searching for a service or product like theirs.

Building a YouTube channel is an easy way to boost visibility on Google — without spending a ton of money on an SEO specialist. Even when a website or blog doesn't rank high in search results, related YouTube videos can.

When you publish a YouTube video about your business, it can appear on the first page of search results as a "suggested video." This is separate from the other search results and so gives you an additional opportunity to gain visibility in Google search results.

Let's look at an example. Imagine a homeowner is searching for someone to install new gutters on their porch. After a quick Google search, they find five comparable companies specializing in gutter installation. The homeowner researches the five companies. They visit the linked websites, read online customer reviews, etc.

In home improvement services, not many small businesses have established a YouTube presence. When the homeowner spots a YouTube video in their Google search results, they are inclined to tune in. This is how the savvy YouTube marketer can stand out online.

Videos add a personal touch to the text-driven landscape of Google results. "Getting to know you" helps establish trust with new customers or clients. This is why word of mouth is such effective marketing.

Now let's take it one step further and imagine that the homeowner finds a video of one business installing gutters last fall. The homeowner can see the company in action and the quality of their work. This business instantly gains credibility and zooms to the top of the homeowner's interest list.

Video marketing outpaces simple websites that only show photos. Furthermore, videos can be repurposed from a website to YouTube and other social media sites. YouTube is versatile. Not only can you use it to publish videos online for free, but you can also embed (i.e., showcase) those videos on other pages of a website, for example, a website's homepage, About, or sales pages.

Embedding a video on a website allows customers to stay on a site while they watch the video. This prevents them from getting distracted by other videos on YouTube. We all know what it feels like to find yourself going down a rabbit hole of cute cat videos. When you embed YouTube videos on your site, you help visitors focus on the amazing things you have to offer by keeping their eyes on your website.

Showcasing embedded YouTube videos on your site also sets you apart from the competition. It's an immediate, engaging advertisement for your business, and it helps grow your YouTube channel. Every video view — including views of embedded videos — gives your YouTube channel more credited watch time.

Anyone with a smartphone can record, edit, and publish quality video content. Yet many businesses still overlook this powerful medium. Below we look at more opportunities to use video across different industries.

Brick-and-Mortar Retail

With little overhead, brick-and-mortar stores can engage customers by showing off what they sell. They can use YouTube videos to elevate their advertising from commonly used outlets like Facebook Marketplace, Craigslist, Letgo, etc., and create a stronger connection with shoppers.

For example, a vintage clothing store might show off their inventory in a short video once per week. They can use the power of YouTube to provide a visual experience for potential customers so that people can see the lush texture and exquisite details of their products.

The weekly videos would promote their business on Google while simultaneously building their YouTube audience. A brick-and-mortar company who also sells online would further benefit by generating more orders as their YouTube audience expands.

Online Retail and Beyond

With YouTube videos, online retailers can one-up typical listings as they appear on Etsy, eBay, and Amazon. They can showcase short videos of products on a separate sales page.

Comparable to the way real estate sites advertise new homes with 360-degree views, online retailers can showcase their inventory using creative videos of their products.

This takes a typical picture-plus-text listing to a whole new level. The retailer can then connect the dots by helping people move seamlessly between viewing a product on YouTube to purchasing it. This is done by adding a link to the relevant sales page on the YouTube videos — thus increasing sales while boosting a YouTube channel's growth.

Building a YouTube audience automatically helps the growth of a YouTube channel and the related business. Loyal YouTube subscribers:

- Buy items online
- View and comment on videos on social media
- Share videos with their friends and network

Gyms and Healthy Living

In 2020 we saw a transition from storefront businesses to online services due to COVID-19. There is opportunity to use YouTube to expand gym and health brands online.

For free or donation-based workout classes, YouTube has advantages over services like Zoom and Skype. When gyms broadcast a workout class using YouTube Live, it strengthens their online presence over the long term.

When they finish a YouTube live stream workout for their customers, they can rebroadcast the live stream on their YouTube channel. Then, existing customers can watch the workout again, and new customers can view it from around the world, adding to the channel's growth (and watch hours).

Additionally, a health business can take advantage of Google's algorithm automatically advertising the video(s) for years to come. Everything uploaded to a YouTube channel gets ranked on Google for SEO purposes.

Service-Based Business

If you have an existing service-based business or want to start one, you need to build your own YouTube channel. Even if you already have a channel, start thinking about how else you can use YouTube to promote your business.

With a YouTube channel, you can introduce yourself to potential clients, for example, by making a channel trailer video that plays automatically when someone visits your channel. This helps people immediately get to know you.

The channel trailer tool allows you to pitch yourself and your services to new viewers. The channel trailer is like a "video pitch." The main difference is that video pitches are personalized for each potential client and kept private, whereas the channel trailer helps you to reach the masses (hundreds or even thousands of people!).

You can have up to two different channel trailers running on your YouTube channel. Customize one to play for "New Visitors," and the other for "Returning Subscribers." This keeps multiple audiences engaged with what you offer.

We discuss channel trailers in more detail in Chapter Six.

YouTube is also structured for communities. You can use YouTube to network with other online service providers in your niche. Take advantage of this by turning your competition into collaboration. Enjoying someone else's videos about being an entrepreneur in the virtual space? Subscribe to their channel.

Inevitably, many of your own YouTube subscribers are also online service providers. Build these into professional relationships and collaborations. They can turn into real-life opportunities.

Finally, as a service provider, you can expand by offering new B2B (Business-to-Business) services. Once you're proficient in YouTube marketing, monetize your skills by helping other online service providers in a different niche.

Established YouTube channels bring credibility. Once you've built your own channel, you can pitch to businesses and offer to create or refurbish their YouTube channels.

Additional Cash Streams From YouTube

As your YouTube channel grows, you have other opportunities to earn revenue from your videos. Most people (with and without YouTube channels) don't know about these tools.

1. Advertising Income

We've already addressed some of the ways that your presence on YouTube can earn a direct income. The most well-known is ad revenue, which you can receive after qualifying for the YouTube Partner Program.

The requirements for the Partner Program are a minimum of 4,000 watch hours plus 1,000 subscribers. After that, you get paid from ads that appear on your videos.

Other methods of earning direct income on YouTube include sponsorships, memberships and Super Chat. We cover the specifics of monetization in Chapter Nine.

2. Education

We touched on this topic above, but it bears repeating. YouTube is an excellent tool for educating people about your brand. Watching a video helps them get to know who you are and what you're about.

You can present videos that introduce and discuss your brand or business. Each video is an opportunity to send traffic back to your website or to get people to check out your products and services.

3. Overall Branding

Whether it's for a new brand or an existing business, your appearance on YouTube solidifies "who you are" in your clients' eyes. YouTube provides the opportunity for consistent and powerful visual branding through logos, animation, and all the visual elements you include on your videos.

Channels can even sell merchandise based on this branding — a t-shirt with a logo, a mug, and more. After you monetize your channel, YouTube has a third-party service that helps you sell merchandise if you choose. Or you can make use of the powerful visual branding on YouTube and sell merchandise direct to your viewers at any point in your YouTube journey.

4. YouTube Live

Live streams allow you to get an instant response from your audience. You can address people directly and chat with them in real time.

You can get feedback from your audience about your business and brand, not to mention the chance to be discovered by new subscribers and drive people back to your website or channel.

The live streams stay active on your channel after you've finished going live. You can monetize existing and future live streams via Google's AdSense advertising program.

Here's another benefit of live streams. When you're running a live stream, anyone watching can donate instantly to your channel. Don't deprive your followers of an opportunity to support you!

5. Live Stream Super Chat

YouTube also features a handy advertising tool called a Live Stream Super Chat — this is a cash token. While you're live on YouTube, other channels can send you a "Super Chat" to advertise themselves.

During your live stream, Super Chats appear in front of you and your YouTube audience in real time. Sending a Super Chat is instant and easy advertising for another YouTube channel. And the cash adds up in your account.

Existing subscribers may also send you Super Chats to say thank you, as a form of tipping, or because they enjoy supporting you on YouTube.

6. Supportive Fans and Memberships

In our experience, YouTube fans are one of the most supportive social media audiences. Now, thanks to YouTube, they can pay you directly for being awesome.

In 2020 YouTube launched its own version of Patreon called memberships. It's a platform for fans to support artists and creators online.

Fans of your channel can show their support by pledging "X" dollar amounts per month. These fan memberships become a recurring source of income for you and your business.

To take advantage of memberships, your channel must qualify for YouTube's Partner Program. This additional revenue is yet another example of how your YouTube audience can become loyal supporters of your brand while also helping your Google search ranking.

Passive Revenue: A YouTube Success Story

I (Lucas) would like to share the story of my friend who has been using YouTube to create a source of passive revenue for his auto repair business.

My buddy is a certified auto mechanic who runs a mechanic shop from his garage in St. Paul, Minnesota. His initial plan was to record the repairs he was already getting paid to do, then upload them to his YouTube channel, "Rust Belt Auto."

After 4,000 hours watched (plus the minimum 1,000 subscribers), "Rust Belt Auto" qualified for YouTube's Partner Program. My friend started earning from the ads running on his YouTube videos. Within a few months, his channel was making over $1,000 per month with ad revenue collected through Google AdSense. And he still had under 2,000 YouTube subscribers.

After two years plus a few months online, his channel now has over 10,000 subscribers and boasts over 3 million views. When he was at 5,000 subscribers, he received around 6,000 daily views on his YouTube channel, just from past videos. His success on YouTube completely surpassed his expectations.

Part of his success comes from his "evergreen" content. Every day, tons of people search Google with questions about auto repairs for DIY projects. Some of them end up finding his instructional YouTube videos.

Not only do these videos advertise his business (he gets new foot traffic as a result, too), but the concept of his channel is simple. He's capturing what he is already doing for work — performing car repairs. And people love it.

His story shows that you don't need to "go viral" to make money on YouTube. My friend had one simple goal and is now adding thousands of dollars to his bank account every month.

Action Step

1. Start a list of the things that you want to get out of YouTube. What kind of channel do you want? Do you want to advertise an existing business or become an influencer within a certain niche? Is your goal to practice your skills and land YouTube marketing clients?

* * *

In the next chapter, we cover the first step in the six-step process to build a profitable YouTube channel. You'll discover why it's necessary to have a strong foundation for your channel. We also share eight video templates so that you can start creating content straight away.

4

CREATE YOUR YOUTUBE PLAN (STEP ONE)

So are you jazzed to get your channel up and running on YouTube? Awesome! The following chapters will help you get there, one step at a time.

First, we cover creating your YouTube plan. Whether you already have a basic concept for your channel or have no idea what your channel will be about, a plan is essential.

Knowing your audience and your objective on YouTube sets you up for success. Your plan provides a clear direction, and when the rubber hits the road, holding on to your goals keeps you thriving.

Choose Your Niche

First things first: what is your YouTube channel about? The overarching topic that you choose is your YouTube niche. As you brainstorm, try to narrow your idea down to one niche. Attempting to appeal to everyone is not a good marketing strategy.

Imagine viewers coming to your channel to learn about DIY sewing tips and then seeing a mix of tax preparation, hiking, and lawn mower repair videos. The DIY sewing crowd is unlikely to return — let alone subscribe — to your channel.

Having a specific audience in mind helps when it comes to tapping the opportunities on YouTube. We call this "niching down."

Niching down involves diving deeper into your niche. It means getting specific about the type of content you're creating. The more specific (and consistent) you are with your content, the faster you grow a large base of supporters and subscribers.

In other words, taking from the previous example, give that DIY sewing crowd the engaging and educational content they want to see.

When you're choosing your niche on YouTube, the sky's the limit. There are YouTube videos and channels for any activity or topic you can imagine. Your YouTube content can be about anything.

But you might be wondering: *Can any niche become profitable?*

If you follow the steps in this book, absolutely! Providing there's an audience interested in your topic, you can start and monetize a YouTube channel around it.

General niches on YouTube include hobbies, leisure, careers, freelancing, entertainment, food, kids, education, and everything in between. Bicycling and coin collecting are niches, as are crocheting, jigsaw puzzles, freelance writing, cute animals, and video editing and oil painting tutorials.

As you're choosing your niche, we want to encourage you to start with what you know.

What do you enjoy in your work or as a hobby?

You can transform anything into interesting content. And simple content ideas can be just as profitable as complex ones. So don't overthink it at this stage.

You could even record part of your daily routine. If you work from home, you could make a time-lapse video of you working and add some fun music. Incorporate some designs and describe the video as "This is what I did today. And I made $X!"

When you come up with an idea, search for it on YouTube using a simple word or phrase. See what YouTube videos are already out there, and in the "suggested videos" category that the search algorithm gives you.

Also search your ideas on Google and pay attention to what videos pop up from YouTube. If there are few suggested videos… then that's a spot you could fill.

However, this doesn't mean you have to find an underserved niche to be successful. Most topics already have an established fan base, and you'll have a sense of that as you see how many views and subscribers existing channels have. An existing audience around a subject indicates that the niche can be profitable. But if you're piggybacking on an already popular idea, make sure you create and upload content that is unique to you.

Some YouTube channels choose their niches based on the creators' comfort — or lack thereof — with being on camera. This is valid; there is room for everyone on YouTube. A high-quality video that contains no talking can be just as effective as one that features you and only you.

Keep this in mind as you read through the following types of YouTube videos that you can create.

Eight Types of YouTube Videos To Create

If you're creating a channel for your business or brand, your YouTube channel is the face of your video marketing strategy. Even if you think your audience is not on YouTube, think again.

YouTube can help you increase awareness and interest — and organically build your following. The following are some types of videos that engage audiences. No matter what niche you choose, you can tailor each one of these to fit your business and offerings.

Note: As you browse your desired niche by searching on YouTube, take note of other video formats (variations of those listed here) that appear repeatedly in your industry.

1. Testimonials

You can make short videos featuring a satisfied customer (or several!). Customer testimonials build trust in your product or service.

2. Product Demonstration

Give the customer more detail about what you're offering with a product demonstration. For virtual service providers, your "product" is your own time and skills. Get creative about showing your fans how you do your work.

3. Tutorial

Uploading tutorials on how to use your products is essential, depending on what you're selling. This represents one of the best kinds of evergreen content. What questions do your customers ask most frequently? Create videos that answer their common questions or that help your customers get the most from your offering.

If you have a service-based or B2B business, a tutorial video might look a little different. You could use it to teach someone how you do one part of your job, or tell them how you got started in the field you're in.

4. Interview a Leader in Your Field

An interview with an interesting person is another approach to building content.

Start with someone who inspires you and makes you think, like a mentor or friend. Offering them a chance to be featured on your channel could benefit them, too (once you've built a following). And it helps build connections with their audience.

5. Project Reviews and Case Studies

In a project review or case study, you can provide a recap of one of your projects and any relevant stats.

While it's great to highlight your successes, you can also tell your audience how you learned from your less-than-successful projects. A balance of both makes you look human.

6. YouTube Live

YouTube Live allows you to engage with your fan base in real time. It's one of the most personal ways to appear on YouTube (and it doesn't allow for editing or redos!). Use this to have a conversation with your fans in real time, and show them your casual side, or an up-close look at one of your events or service offerings.

There is an infinite number of things you can do with YouTube Live. We discuss this in more detail in Chapter Eight.

7. Video Blogs (Vlogs)

A vlog is content that you would write a blog post on, but instead you talk to the camera about it. You can use video blogs to create content around your daily life, work, and routine, for example, by recording a vlog series with daily or weekly videos about a new project you are working on.

8. Live Events

Video evidence of live events, such as conferences, speakers, lectures, and concerts, is excellent content for YouTube. These videos provide proof of your business on the ground. Plus, hearing the cheers of a live audience is exciting.

Brainstorm Content

Now you have a niche and understand the types of videos you can create, it's time to brainstorm your initial content.

Think about your target market and your main objective. We recommend writing out a brief description of your niche and your number one goal for your channel. Keep this nearby to remind you of what you want to achieve and whom you're creating your channel for.

With your target audience in mind, set aside time to brainstorm content. No distractions, no editing your ideas. Throw it all out on the table. Compile a master list of ideas you can use over the coming weeks or months.

After this monthly (or bimonthly) brain dump, let it simmer. When you come back to the list, you can select the ideas that most excite you or refine them and make them shine. If you want help deciding between a list of awesome video ideas, you could poll an existing audience on another social platform.

Your content brainstorming sessions are an opportunity to ask yourself what your video marketing strategy is. When it comes to choosing the format of your videos, return to the "Eight Types of YouTube Videos to Create" in the previous section, and make a short list of the formats that are most relevant to you or your business.

Ultimately, your marketing strategy should revolve around the goals and values of your business. People want to know who you are, what you're doing, and why you're doing it. And if your business has one or more physical locations, then your audience should know where you are as well.

Make sure you include:

- The "Why" behind your business
- Specific service or product offerings
- Geographic location (if you have a physical storefront)

You should consider all this information as the "evergreen" content on your channel. We cover evergreen versus time-sensitive content later in this chapter.

Develop Subcategories in Your Niche

When it comes to content, you have one central theme — this is your chosen niche. But each niche features many subcategories. Having some variety within your niche keeps viewers wanting more on YouTube. No one wants to watch the same video over and over.

These subcategories are what you want to explore in each of your videos. Think of it as a mind map: the main niche is the central point. But there are multiple related concepts that branch out from there.

Take some time in your brainstorming session to list possible subcategories in your niche. For example, if personal finance is your main theme, your subcategories could include:

- Retirement
- Education planning
- Small business
- Cash reserves
- Debt payoff
- Money mindset
- Employment
- Side hustles
- Investing

As you create this list, think about your audience and what topics would interest them when they arrive at your channel and want to learn more about your niche and goal.

Evergreen vs. Time-Sensitive Content

Evergreen content remains popular over the long term. It is the opposite of time-sensitive content.

We recommend focusing on evergreen content. Chasing short-term trends can cause spikes in your channel's popularity. However, evergreen content enjoys a slow and steady rise. Get in at the bottom, create quality content that doesn't go stale, and watch your metrics climb.

Examples of evergreen content include things that people always want to know, from the practical and instructive ("how to change a flat tire") to the perennially entertaining ("cats playing in boxes").

Time-sensitive content, on the other hand, can go viral quickly, but then it dies down in popularity. Examples of time-sensitive content include videos related to current events and pop culture trends. Anything that can become outdated is time-sensitive.

As you're planning your content, be aware of whether you're leaning towards evergreen or time-sensitive. If possible, ensure that all — or at least most — of your content is evergreen.

Evergreen content can still include date information. Let's say you're vlogging about training for a fitness competition. Including dates in your videos is essential. This doesn't cause your videos to become stale because the dates are relevant to show progress in training (e.g., "one month out").

More examples of evergreen content are tutorials, educational topics, DIY topics, testimonials, and many vlogs. Of course, you can later revise your evergreen content to make sure it stays up-to-date, but you don't want all your videos to be losing relevancy over time.

If you want your channel to take advantage of current events or viral trends, verify that this is a viable strategy for you. Monitoring your subscriber conversion rate from those videos tells you if this is a good approach to grow your channel.

When it comes to SEO (search engine optimization), for time-sensitive content, avoid tagging current events. This doesn't help you gain popularity, as there's simply too much competition for those tags.

We discuss SEO in more detail in Chapter Six.

Editorial Calendar

Finally, you need a place for all the polished video ideas you come up with. This is the role of the editorial calendar.

While those messy brainstorming notebooks are useful for future reference (whenever ideas run dry), the editorial calendar keeps you on track. It tells you exactly what content you're publishing on YouTube, and when.

Your editorial calendar should include the following:

- Video content ideas for the next few weeks.
- When you plan to post each video (pick a consistent schedule that you can commit to).

We recommend using a planner like Trello or CoSchedule to write down your schedule and then sticking with it.

As you gain experience and get to know your target audience, keep your editorial calendar full for a minimum of one month ahead. Ideally, you want to have content ready for the next 3-6 months. This takes some of the pressure off publishing. You can work up to this goal at a pace that works for you.

As you create your editorial calendar, allow time in the master schedule to brainstorm, shoot videos, edit footage, and publish.

The structure of your editorial calendar is dependent on how often you post and the length of your content. If you're starting a brand-new YouTube channel, we recommend uploading videos that are 3-10 minutes in length. A standard length is 5-7 minutes.

As for how frequently you should post, start with at least one video every two weeks, and preferably, one video every week. The goal is two to three videos per week if you want to maximize your growth. No matter what you choose, be consistent. Don't overreach and then miss the deadlines you committed to.

When you keep to a consistent schedule, your channel experiences faster organic growth.

Be Real, Be Yourself

When you present yourself on YouTube, as an individual or as a brand, you can choose what to share and what not to share. But remember these two things:

Be real and be yourself.

By aligning with your own values, you find your unique "voice." And as a result, people who share your values are drawn to your channel, and your audience grows quickly and easily.

Also follow these general rules of thumb to boost your success (and trust in your brand) on YouTube:

1. Create Original Content

While you're browsing your niche, be aware of what other content creators are doing, but don't copy them.

Giving viewers the exact same content might be tempting, especially if the original content has millions of views, but don't do it. It's not cool. Plus, you could be booted from Google's search algorithm if they discover plagiarized content.

YouTube viewers are easily disappointed when content is repetitive and uncreative. They want something new. Even though it's harder to be creative than to copy someone else, it's the right thing to do. And it drives more subscribers to you in the long run.

2. Don't Exaggerate Content

Be real about your content and what you say on your channel. If you are being fake, people read through that, especially on live stream.

We promise that it's much easier to be the person you are rather than trying to be someone else. Video as a medium encourages human-to-human connection. People can show their vulnerability, and their strengths and weaknesses. On YouTube, if you prove yourself to be human, you're guaranteed brand loyalty.

3. Don't Do Stupid Things in Public

Once you have a public profile and a following of hundreds or thousands (or millions!) of people, you have a lot of eyes watching you. There are many stories of successful YouTube channels that tanked because the people behind them made bad decisions in their personal lives.

As an online "influencer," you are just that. You influence people, but you are responsible for keeping your own actions in check. People are looking up to you.

YouTube is also watching you. You must stay within their Community Guidelines. (Stay up-to-date with these and read them regularly.) YouTube can flag your channel at any point if it doesn't meet their guidelines.

Ultimately, keep your channel original, respectful, and professional.

Step One Summary

Let's recap everything we covered in this chapter. Here are the things you should do to create your YouTube plan:

- Choose your niche.
- Research your niche on YouTube and Google. Who is your target audience?
- Brainstorm your video marketing strategy. Make a list of what potential customers need to know about your business, and how you'll transform that into video.
- Brainstorm the types of YouTube videos you want to feature on your channel.
- Brainstorm your content and subcategories.
- Identify your "evergreen" content. Plan content that stays relevant long-term.

- Create your editorial calendar. Enter video ideas and publishing dates.
- Be real, be kind, and remember to follow YouTube's community guidelines.

There's room for everyone on YouTube, so be yourself! Don't limit yourself to niches that you believe are the most "marketable." Do pay attention to what you actually want to do, your audience, your target goals on YouTube, and the quality of your content.

Sound good? You got this!

Action Steps

1. Brainstorm your niche and come up with a list of five to 10 subcategories.

2. Review your subcategories and use the ones that "pop out" at you as inspiration to brainstorm three video ideas.

* * *

Next, you will set up your Google account and YouTube channel. We show you how to make your channel stand out by optimizing your channel art, your round logo, and your banner. Once you've filled out your YouTube profile, you'll be ready to make your first video and publish it in Chapter Six. Get pumped!

5

SET UP YOUR YOUTUBE ACCOUNT (STEP TWO)

You've brainstormed the niche and content for your new channel. Now it's time to set up your YouTube account. In this chapter we cover everything you need, starting with the basics. We show you how to create a professional-looking YouTube channel page. Let's get started.

Start With a Google Account

Before you create a YouTube channel, you need a Google account. If you already have an email account with Google (i.e., Gmail), use it to sign in to YouTube. If you don't have one already, you can create one by visiting YouTube.com and clicking "Sign in." Then, follow the onscreen instructions.

When creating a new Google account on YouTube, you're asked whether you are using a personal account or brand account. A personal account is one that only you will manage, and it shares your name and photo on your Google account. A brand account can be managed by multiple owners or managers. Brand accounts can have a different name and photo from your Google account. If you aren't sure what name and photo you want to choose yet, start with a brand account.

Your next step is to create a YouTube channel. Having a Google account lets you interact on YouTube — you can like and subscribe to other people's videos — but if you want to upload your own content, then you also need a YouTube channel.

Finally, follow the prompts to verify your YouTube account. You need a working phone number to do this.

Note: If you make a new Google account before you create your YouTube channel, consider creating an email address that matches your channel name (which we get to next). This gives you consistent branding, especially if you anticipate using your email to interact with viewers, fans, and other channels. It also simplifies your life, since you keep a separate inbox for your channel-related communication.

Name Your Channel

If you're linking an existing Google account with your new YouTube channel (and you've chosen to create a personal account), you'll notice that your name and profile image have migrated over from Google into your YouTube account. The only way to change these is through Google accounts.

But if you're setting up a new Google account, or if you're setting up a brand account on YouTube, you can choose a name for your YouTube channel. Take a minute to select a name that reflects your business. If you're building a personal brand, you can use your own name. If your channel is promoting a project or product, incorporate that as concisely as you can.

Your goal is to choose a name that is short and memorable, and tells us what your channel is all about.

Create a Round Logo

Be sure to put some thought in to your round logo (aka channel icon), but don't get stuck here. You must get this right because your round logo, along with your channel name, appears below every video you upload and every comment you make. You want to make a good impression when viewers first see you.

Below are three questions to help you create a compelling logo. You'll use these same criteria for the entire "look" of your channel.

- Message: Does your logo reflect what your YouTube channel is all about?
- Clarity: If you have text, is it easy to read when the logo is much smaller in size?
- Aesthetics: Is your logo visually appealing?

As you create your custom visual branding in YouTube, remember to be consistent in terms of style, color, verbal tone, etc. The more visually consistent, the more memorable your brand.

If you're thinking, *How do I do this? I want to make videos, not be a graphic designer!* — don't worry. You can draw up something simple with a tool like Canva, or you can hire custom artwork from affordable freelancer websites like Fiverr and 99designs. If you hire out, be ready to tell your designer the look and feel you want.

Choose Your Channel Art

Your channel art is the banner that appears at the top of your YouTube page. It's the first thing people see when they visit your channel, even before they watch any videos. Your channel art must fit with the rest of your brand. You can do this by simply picking one or two colors and one or two fonts for all your branding.

Also, make sure that each piece of your visual branding is high quality, and fits the desktop, mobile app, and iPad versions of YouTube.

That's why image sizing and optimization are so important. Familiarize yourself with the rules about optimum sizing and layout for the round logo and channel art. You can find all the details on the YouTube help pages.[1]

If you're looking for images, start with some copyright-free stock photos. You can layer your own designs or text over these photos. As with your round logo, you can use Canva to create your own channel art or hire a freelancer via a marketplace like Fiverr or 99designs.

Note: You can edit and replace your channel art on your YouTube channel at any point. While you should choose and upload channel art as you're setting up your YouTube account, bear in mind that you can always improve your images later.

Complete Your YouTube Profile

Now that you've set up the visual elements of your YouTube channel, let's focus on the rest of your homepage. Be ready to answer the question: what is your channel about?

Your channel homepage appears when someone clicks on the name of your YouTube channel. Think of this page as a basic website. Just like a professional website, it contains all the essential information about your brand.

First, fill out your About page, which can be found on the rightmost tab of your YouTube channel homepage. Your About page should contain all the specifics about your brand.

In the "Description" area on the About page, write a few short paragraphs about who you are, what you're doing on YouTube, and why they should follow you. Be concise — you don't need to write a novel. Some people include links in this section, although these links must be written in full, starting with "https://www...."

Below the description, there's another location to provide links back to your professional website, social media profiles, and other pages that you want to promote. These embedded links are a clean way to present external branding that represents you and your relevant projects.

Among the embedded links, you can also include a link to your PayPal page. This allows customers to pay you directly for products or services that you sell on YouTube.

At the bottom of the About page, you can add your email address for your viewers to get in touch. When you set your email address to "public," you definitely get mail, so be prepared! People want to connect with you on a human level after watching your videos. And it can even lead to business connections down the line.

Finally, give your channel homepage a read-through for mistakes or accidents in image sizing. There's no limit to the number of times you can edit this page, so keep all the information up-to-date.

The YouTube Studio

We'd like to introduce you to a helpful and free tool: the YouTube Studio. Knowing how to use the YouTube Studio is just as important as finding your way around your YouTube channel homepage. It's that useful!

The YouTube Studio allows you to customize every aspect of your videos, including:

- curating playlists
- adding custom thumbnails, end screens, and info cards
- editing and adding music to videos
- viewing analytics and monetization
- starting a live stream

This tool helps you make high-quality content right out of the gate. So make the most of these built-in tools that YouTube offers. You can navigate to the studio by selecting your profile picture in the top right, then selecting YouTube Studio.

Step Two Summary

Feeling good? Here's a summary of how far you've come in this chapter. You should now know how to:

- Start a YouTube channel by connecting an existing Google account or creating a new Google account.
- Choose your channel name and think about branding.
- Create your channel icon (round logo) and channel art.
- Fill out your YouTube homepage, with a focus on the About page. This includes your description, links, and email address if you want.
- Explore YouTube Studio and get familiar with some of the useful tools that help streamline your time spent on YouTube.

Action Steps

1. Brainstorm a name and round logo for your channel.

2. Create a YouTube account by starting a new Google account or connecting an existing one, and add your name and logo.

3. Create your channel art and fill out your YouTube profile.

* * *

Okay, it's time to bring your video ideas to life. In Chapter Six, you'll be recording, uploading, and optimizing your first three videos. Piece of cake, right? This is the meat of the YouTube process and there's a lot to learn. But don't worry, we break it down step-by-step.

6

RECORD YOUR FIRST THREE VIDEOS (STEP THREE)

In this chapter we guide you through creating your first videos, from planning to publishing. There's a lot of information here, and all of it is useful. Take your time, write notes, and don't get discouraged. Keep moving forward, even if you don't catch all the details the first time you read this. For future videos, you can review this chapter, add some finesse, and level up your YouTube game.

We start by planning your initial content, drawing on the brainstorming you did in previous chapters. Then, we explain the technical setup so that you can shoot quality videos from the start (no fancy equipment necessary!).

After that, we help you refine your content using a basic YouTube video template, which ensures that you have all the right elements to engage viewers, especially the call to action. Then, we talk about editing and uploading, including the best tools for editing within the YouTube Studio.

We also dip our toes into search engine optimization (SEO). SEO can sound intimidating, but we break it down for you into a few simple steps. We show you how to optimize your videos by creating a list of relevant keywords and using them to craft specific video titles, descriptions, and tags.

Finally, we cover the basic settings for publishing your video and discuss the channel trailer, which we mentioned in Chapter Three.

Plan Your Initial Content

Let's be honest: creating videos can be intimidating. It's a complicated process, from planning to shooting, to editing and uploading. That's why, for your first three videos, try to simplify each step. To start with, focus on the following:

- Keep each video short (3-5 minutes). It doesn't need to be long, but it does need to be interesting.
- For your content, focus on a topic you're familiar with in your chosen niche.
- Keep it low-risk. This video doesn't have to be the end-all-be-all introduction to who you are. (You can tackle that when you get more comfortable with your goals.)
- Keep the production simple. The goal is to shoot, edit, and upload each video as soon as possible. It's enough to showcase yourself talking.
- Optional: Choose something "visual" to guide your content. You can add footage (videos or still images) that tells a story or proves your point in a simple, direct way.

Remember from Chapter Four that there are eight types of videos you can create, including testimonials, tutorials, interviews, and video blogs (vlogs). And within your niche, you have a number of subcategories to explore. As you brainstorm your first three video concepts, choose from the previous list of video types and pick one subcategory.

While you're planning, ask yourself:

Do my video concepts further my channel goal?

Are they geared towards my target audience?

Don't be afraid to go back and revise your ideas until they reflect your goals. And remember to focus on evergreen content for these initial videos.

Technical Setup

When you think of pro YouTubers, you might picture their studios, filled with expensive cameras, tripods, and lights. But you don't need to invest in fancy equipment, videographers, or stage sets. We promise. As long as you have a phone camera, computer webcam, or similar device that takes a good-quality video, you have enough to get started.

Here are our tips for creating quality videos on a budget.

Focus on what you see:

- Choose a basic background for shooting your video that isn't distracting or ugly.
- Make sure there's enough light on you (or whoever is in focus), so that you can clearly be seen.
- Hold the camera still. If it's resting on a table or other stationary object, even better.
- Make yourself look presentable. Especially if you're trying to build your personal brand, take a minute to comb your hair and put on a clean shirt!

Focus on what you hear:

- Listen for background noise in the area where you plan to shoot, and record in a quiet spot or room if possible. The bottom line is that we should be able to hear your voice clearly.
- Record a short take as a test run to check your voice isn't too quiet or too loud. A crunching and distorted sound in the

playback means you're maxing out your microphone and need to turn your volume down by a few clicks.

Camera orientation:

- Always record your videos for YouTube in landscape mode. That's a 16:9 aspect ratio, for you techies out there. This means you need to hold your phone horizontally if you're recording on a phone camera. If you take videos in portrait mode (vertically), you miss out on a lot of visual space on YouTube, not to mention that YouTube viewers have little patience with clunky videos.

Video Template

Now let's explore the elements of a successful YouTube video, so you can have a template to use while you're shooting. This video template transcends genre. Whether you're delivering toy reviews, talking about blogging, giving DIY tips, or comparing different brands of wood glue, your YouTube videos will benefit from this basic template.

If you're talking in the video, keep your tone friendly and casual, and be concise. If you prefer, you can write out a script beforehand, and practice to make sure it's the right length. If you do this, be engaging and read it like a human (and look at the camera).

The video template has four components: intro, meat, call to action, and end screen.

Intro

Start by introducing yourself and what the video is about. In the editing process, you can also add a simple title screen containing the title (and subtitle, if relevant) of your video. However, it's still a good idea to introduce the topic verbally.

Meat

After the intro, get into the "meat" of your video. Ask yourself, *What* would the viewer want to know about me or my topic? And then answer those questions. This is the most substantial section.

Call To Action (CTA)

Include an "ask" at the end of every video you make. This is the call to action (CTA) for your viewers. You have your audience's attention: now what do you want them to do? Let them know.

For example, ask them to like, comment, and subscribe to build engagement with your channel and increase your subscriber list. When you deliver this call to action, be sure to wait until the end of the video. Viewers want to see what you have to offer before they "subscribe" and "like."

End Screen

Your end screen is the final portion of your video. It's there to reinforce that call to action and direct your viewer to other videos on your channel. You add the end screen graphics during the editing stage. But while you're still rolling, add some "filler" footage at the end of your video. This is not supposed to be anything important. This filler acts as a background for the graphics you layer on top later. Give yourself 20-25 seconds of filler footage.

These are the basic elements of a YouTube video. As you make your own videos, you'll develop a more specific template that works for you and your niche. Pay attention to the comments, too. Viewers give feedback, and if you've left something out, you're likely to hear about it! Be responsive to feedback and eager to learn, and your content will keep improving.

Speaking of video templates and timing, we recommend tuning in to popular channels in your niche. Take notes on their videos. What worked? What kept your attention? Don't copy their content word for word; rather, adopt a bird's-eye view and get a sense of their tone and timing. Pay attention to:

- How do they introduce themselves? Is it formal or informal?

- How long is their intro? (In seconds or minutes)
- How and when did they present their CTA?
- How long did their CTA take?
- What works (or doesn't work) about the "watch next" features on their end screen?

By analyzing other people's videos and learning from their successes, you create your own successful channel.

Edit and Upload

After recording your video footage, your next step is editing. We recommend using a free third-party editing software app, such as iMovie. Don't waste your money and time buying any fancy software until you're established on YouTube.

We're keeping the editing simple for these first three videos. Don't get bogged down here. Consider your overall video length. Aim for 3-5 minutes. If any part of your video feels like it's getting offtrack or going too long, then cut it. If you sneezed or broke out into giggles, you can cut those moments too. Always keep the purpose of your video in mind.

While editing, think about your background audio. Would music lighten things up and fill empty space? You can add music during editing. Or you can add music after you upload using YouTube's library of copyright-free music. If you add music, take care not to cover up your voice if the video features you talking.

And remember to keep those final 20-25 seconds of "filler" footage we mentioned. You need that time for your end screen, which you add using YouTube Studio after uploading the video file. We explain more on that below.

Finally, watch your video through one last time to check you haven't missed something.

At this point, you've made all the changes you want to your video.

Once you upload the file, there is no more editing outside of YouTube. The next step is to get your video uploaded and processed. After uploading, the "processing" happens on its own, without you having to do anything.

Finalize in YouTube Studio

When your video is processed, you finalize your video in YouTube Studio. This is where you can add end screens, cards, and thumbnails to your videos. These elements make your videos more visually appealing and give them a professional appearance.

Let's do a deeper dive into the end screen. You've already created a background of 20-25 seconds for your end screen at the end of your video. Next you layer graphics of your other videos, your round logo, and a link to subscribe to your channel. Remember that the end screen should accomplish two things:

1. Reinforce your CTA.

Use some text to tell people to like, comment, and subscribe. Don't forget to include a link or button to subscribe to your channel.

2. Tell the viewer what to watch next.

Once your channel has more than one video, add your own "watch next" videos in the end screen. This keeps people on your channel. If someone likes a video, they may want to see more. Make that as easy as possible for them by displaying a list of your other videos (on related subjects, if possible).

Put as much information as will fit in the frame of the end screen, within reason! Keep it there for about 20 seconds, giving the viewer time to read and process everything.

Your end screen can be as fancy or as simple as you want. I (Lucas) like to jazz up my end screens with some animation. My end screens have bright colors and fun arrows, pointing out the next videos to watch and how to subscribe. This is something you can add as you gain fluency in creating graphics.

Cards are an advanced feature that you should use as soon as you're comfortable with YouTube Studio. Cards are tiny links that appear in your video while someone is watching, and they can link to other videos, other channels, your own channel, or external links, such as your website. They can also link to "donations" and "polls," which are more advanced features.

In YouTube Studio, you can add cards, which show up in the upper right of the video, like a notification. When the viewer clicks on the card, it takes them to the link you've added.

Cards work best when they're responding to something you've just said in your video. If you take 20 seconds to explain why people should donate to a project, include a card at that point in the video which leads them to the "donate" webpage.

Cards are just one example of how to use your videos to encourage immediate viewer feedback or draw potential customers into a sales funnel.

For visual clarity, don't use cards during your end screen. When you're done adding cards and an end screen, watch your video again — all of it — to make sure it appears how you want.

Video Thumbnails

At this point, add a custom thumbnail to your video. As this is the first image your viewers see when they're scrolling through a list of videos, thumbnails are important. The thumbnail and the video title are what determines whether someone clicks on your video to watch it.

YouTube offers you a list of still images from your video to use as thumbnail options. But we recommend making your own. It turns out that 90% of the most popular videos on YouTube have custom thumbnails.[1] So let's hop on that custom thumbnail train.

Create a thumbnail image that fits the following criteria. You can use a free tool like Canva to do this.

- Format: Landscape mode, or 16:9 aspect ratio
- File type: .jpg or .png
- High resolution: Around 2 MB. (It shouldn't be blurry.)
- Think about scale. Is your image clear when it's scaled down, for example, when someone scrolls past it in a list of videos? Close-up images work well when scaled down.
- Optional: Overlay text on your image. Make any text clear and bold. It must be readable when the image is scaled down. Aim for as few words as possible: six words maximum.

Optimize for Search

When you finish adding the end screen, cards, and thumbnail, you want to incorporate relevant keywords into the title, description, and tags of your videos. Keywords are the terms that people search for on Google or YouTube, like "best running shoes," for instance. This is an essential step in getting your video to appear on search engines.

Many people use YouTube as a search engine, just like they use Google. They search for anything, from how to load a moving truck to DIY picture frames. The most popular keywords tell you what people are thinking about. Keywords reflect people's real questions, interests, and needs.

Once you've created compelling videos, you want people to see them. Without using keywords, it's like only doing the job halfway — you won't see as many results for your effort.

Look for keywords that help you appear near the top of search engine results and promote a "good user experience." Your keywords should strike a balance between the following:

- Your keywords meet a need, meaning they're not too general and not too specific. Focus on keywords that are searched by

an average of 10,000 people each month (in a moment we show you how to use a keyword tool to discover this information).
- Your keywords have low competition, i.e., your competitors haven't yet answered people's questions about the topic.
- Your keywords are relevant to your content. People have a "good user experience" when their search questions are answered, that is, when the keywords (the questions) relate to the content you've published (the answers).

Under one niche or topic, there are thousands of keywords and keyword variations that can describe your topic. Imagine you create videos in the gardening niche. "Gardening" is a competitive term because of how general it is. But here are eight more specific and less competitive keywords within the subcategory "growing your own food:"

- Urban farming
- City farming
- Starting a community garden
- Grow food indoors
- Starting tomatoes indoors
- What vegetables should be planted together
- Keep chickens cool in summer
- City composting
- Homemade organic fertilizer

When you come up with a list of related search terms (keywords), try to put yourself in the shoes of the person searching. What are the possible questions they might have about the topic? And based on their interest in that topic, what other interests or questions do they probably have?

Now create your own list of eight (or so) keywords. Start by breaking down what your content is about, for both your channel and your individual videos. After brainstorming keywords and topics, plug them into a keyword tool. The software shows you how many people are searching those terms and their ranking difficulty (less competitive is better). It even gives you other keyword ideas you hadn't thought about.

Here are some examples of keyword software to try:

- Google Keyword Planner: Free with Google Ads account (which is itself free to sign up for). It displays a list of keyword ideas based on your initial keyword.
- Keyword Generator: This free software generates up to 150 search terms based on your initial entry.
- TubeBuddy: A paid service that's designed for YouTubers. It even auto-suggests keywords while you're editing and publishing your video and lists the competitiveness of those keywords. But we recommend starting out with one of the free services first.

Once you have a list of keywords that are consistent with your channel topic, use these on every video you publish. For each specific video, add one or two extra keywords to describe the content for that specific video.

Doing the research to find your first eight keywords is the starting point. But even if you're covering evergreen content, internet trends and the competitiveness of keywords change over time. Be sure to analyze your keywords at least annually. Quarterly is best. In the future, you can replace your keywords as you fine-tune your niche.

Note: Within YouTube Studio, there's a page that shows your most successful keywords. Using this helps you gauge your growth based on keywords.

Alright, you've got your list of keywords — now what?

Once you've found keywords that are relevant to your channel, integrate those keywords into your video title, description, and tags. The goal here is to use them naturally. Never "stuff" your keywords where they don't make grammatical or topical sense.

Remember that keywords are based on "good user experience," i.e., did the people who searched for that keyword find what they were looking for?

Include your target keywords in all three locations on your videos: the title, description, and tags. Here's how to integrate those keywords into each of these locations.

1. Video Title

Write a title that accurately describes the content of your video. Then, refine your title to incorporate your target keywords. Keep the title short, up to 60 characters.

2. Video Description

Describe your video accurately and concisely. Capture the critical information in the first two to three lines of text, or approximately 100 characters. After that, the viewer must click "read more" to read the rest of your description. After those first two to three lines, copy your video title into your video description. This ensures that you're maximizing your keyword density.

3. Video Tags

Next, add three tags to your video. A "tag" is simply a keyword in a hashtag (#). It tells people — and search engines — what your video is about.

Tags work as single words or short phrases. You can duplicate relevant keywords from your video title without the small words like "of" and "the." As with the video description, start with your highest-priority tags, and only use tags that are relevant to your content.

Also consider tagging locations on your video. This can further help with search rankings, especially if you have a business that serves local customers. For example, you can include your town or city name as a tag.

To boost your SEO rankings even more, mention your keywords naturally within your video itself. Do this on every video you make. Let's say a YouTube team member does a manual review of your channel. If they hear you talking about your keywords, then you're good to go. YouTube wants to ensure that you're using keywords that relate to your channel and videos.

Pro tip: Your YouTube channel, not just individual videos, can benefit from SEO. Incorporate tags (keywords) that describe your niche and subcategories into your channel description. When people search those keywords, your channel appears in the results. Use the number one topic you're exploring in your channel as your first tag in the list.

Publishing

When you upload your videos, be aware of your video settings. For the first few videos (at least), select "Publish as Public." This means that your video is available for free everywhere on the search engines, YouTube and Google. When a video is set to "public," it is viewable on your channel page too.

But "public mode" isn't the only option. In the future, you can take advantage of some other options. Publishing videos as "private" means that only you can see them. But at any point, you can change these settings so that your "private" videos become "public" (and vice versa).

As you're preparing to publish content, you can upload finished videos and keep them in private mode. Once you have four or five videos ready, you can publish them as public according to the publishing schedule you've made on your editorial calendar.

Thanks to the "scheduling" function in the YouTube Studio, you can choose the date and time when each video set to private will be published. Once you get your rhythm, consider keeping four to six videos on the deck, ready to publish to your channel. This helps you stick to a consistent schedule without burning out.

How do you know what time of day to publish? Choosing exactly when new content goes live depends on your time zone. Aim to publish content when your target audience is most likely to see your video, i.e., when they're awake. Publishing in the morning is an effective strategy, since it gives your audience the entire day to discover and share your content.

For me (Lucas), publishing at 9 a.m. CDT works well. Other people have found success publishing regularly at noon, or in the afternoon. Whatever time you choose, be consistent with it. And use the scheduling tool so you don't have to remember to push a button at 9 a.m., or whatever time you've chosen.

Once you learn the steps, keeping up with your editorial calendar is easy. And again — commit to your schedule. After a while, your fans expect a video to drop on particular days and times. The last thing you want is for fans to be waiting for a video that never appears. Don't let them down, and don't lose their views. Publish regularly, no matter what, and you will enjoy organic growth.

Channel Trailer

After a few months of uploading videos regularly, the next step in optimizing your channel is setting up a channel trailer. We discussed the potential for marketing via channel trailers in Chapter Three. The channel trailer is the video that plays automatically when people visit your channel. It's an opportunity to share what your channel is all about.

Compare the views on your videos and set your most popular video as your channel trailer. Later, you can decide if you want to make a specific trailer video. Channel trailers feature the channel and its creator. They can be a buzzed-up introduction, saying, "Hey, this is me, this is what my channel is about," and give some personalized insight into who you are as a person.

The structure for a channel trailer is the same as the basic video template we described earlier in this chapter. It should include an introduction, some substance in the middle, and a call to action at the end, followed by an end screen.

Step Three Summary

We've covered a lot of detail in this chapter. Give yourself a high five because this is a lot of information to process. Following these steps helps you feel confident as you make your first three videos and gives you a solid foundation for creating future YouTube videos.

Let's summarize the mountain we climbed:

- Plan out your initial content. Simplify your process and keep your videos short. Focus on a topic you're familiar with and don't overcomplicate the production. Your video topics should reflect the goal of your channel. Remember to keep your target audience in mind.
- Focus on your technical setup. Record your videos in landscape mode. Find a non-distracting video background in a spot with minimal background noise. Do a test run to check for audio levels and to make sure the subject has enough light.
- Edit your videos. Use a third-party movie editing app, like iMovie, to edit your footage together. Keep your videos to 3-5 minutes. Add music if necessary. Then, watch the whole video to check you haven't missed anything.
- Upload your videos to YouTube and enter YouTube Studio. Once you're there, add an end screen, cards, and a custom video thumbnail.
- Optimize your videos for search on YouTube by including relevant keywords in the title, description, and tags.
- Publish your videos. Set your first few videos to publish as "public" so that they appear in the search results. Create a publishing schedule and stick to it.
- Add a channel trailer. After two months of regular uploads, set your most popular video as your channel trailer. You can

also make a video specifically designed to welcome folks to your channel.

If you follow these steps, your channel will grow. Be consistent, and people will want to invest in your brand by subscribing and following you. With interesting videos, consistency, and persistence, you can't lose.

Action Steps

1. Plan and record your first video on your mobile device or the best camera you have available. Record it in "landscape" mode and keep it to 3-5 minutes.

2. Jot down two to three search terms (keywords) that describe the topic of your channel or video. Using keyword generating software, come up with a list of eight more keywords that are low competition and high volume (about 10,000 monthly searches). Integrate your most relevant keywords into your video title, description, and tags.

3. Once you've edited and uploaded your video and added a thumbnail, title, description, and tags, publish it as "public." You can also schedule it to be published at a specific time of day when your audience will be most likely to see it.

* * *

Now that you're set with an optimized channel page and three videos to be proud of, you're ready to share your work with the world, starting with your family and friends. And yes, if you'd rather grow in anonymity, we have tips for you as well. Get ready: we're making your YouTube channel happen.

7

LAUNCH YOUR CHANNEL (STEP FOUR)

In the previous chapter, you created your first compelling content on YouTube, which is more than half the battle. The next step to YouTube success is building your subscriber list. Because what's the point of having amazing content if no one sees it? Plus, the more subscribers and views your channel has, the closer it is to monetization.

In this chapter we share a framework for launching your channel on social media. We also discuss implementing social media to consistently grow your channel down the line. But there are other strategies to accomplish growth, even if you don't use social media. The bottom line: we're going outside of YouTube to build your YouTube channel.

Launching your channel is a point of departure, and the strategies we share are building blocks. You will add more marketing channels to your arsenal as you become comfortable promoting your brand. We discuss more strategies to grow your following in Chapter Eight. For now, focus on getting yourself out there. From sharing on social media to in-person discussions to email lists, we know that if you promote yourself regularly, your channel will see steady, organic growth.

So let's get started and launch your YouTube channel!

Promote Yourself Everywhere

Now that you've uploaded three videos, it's time to spread the word. Here are a few questions you might be wondering about promoting your channel.

Where is the best place to promote myself?

Everywhere you feel comfortable doing so! In this chapter we cover promoting your channel and videos on social media platforms, email newsletters, and more. We also discuss some of the potential in video marketing and how you can promote your brand and your channel simultaneously.

What if my first three videos aren't that great?

Every YouTube channel started out with imperfections; we promise. Creating video content is a learning curve. But even if you don't feel "ready," it's time to push forward, promote, and keep on producing more videos. With practice, you'll get more comfortable and skilled.

Successful YouTube channels never let their imperfections slow them down, and they improve over time. In fact, we've seen many channels turn their earliest, cringe-worthy videos into popular content later on. Why? In order to showcase just how far they've come. It's inspiring to watch these videos, because they are proof that regular people can dig into their skill set, improve, and gain confidence.

Why is promoting myself important?

Promoting yourself is one easy method to gain subscribers, and there are added benefits as well. Posting your videos on social media platforms where you have an existing following increases your channel's visibility on Google. As we explained in Chapter Three, search engine optimization, i.e., improving your ranking results via search engines, is essential. Remember, the name of the game is making it easy for people to discover your channel.

Share on Social Media

The first step in launching your YouTube channel is to leverage your existing social media accounts. You can gain subscribers from your existing network: your clients, colleagues, friends, and family. If you have personal and business pages on Facebook or other platforms, use both to promote your channel.

Start by announcing the launch of your channel and link to your first video. Encourage people to subscribe. Then, announce each successive video you publish as soon as it goes live on YouTube. If you can, upload a short teaser of the video, for example, upload a portion of the video to Facebook or Instagram.

Announcing each YouTube video on Twitter, Instagram, Facebook, Pinterest, etc.... You might be thinking, *This is time-consuming work, right? Is it even worth it?*

It's absolutely worthwhile, and we have tips to save you time on these social media blasts. Remember your goal here: to get subscriptions. By posting announcements on social media, you can drive more traffic to your channel, gain subscriptions, and improve your SEO.

Unless you only use one form of social media, we don't recommend doing each post manually. That can drain your time. Instead, there are tools like Buffer to help you post to multiple social media accounts at once. Take advantage of these time-saving tools to streamline your process.

And while we're talking about scheduling, go ahead and take out your editorial calendar. It's time to add social media blasts. Enter your social media schedule around your YouTube publishing schedule. To maximize views, it's best to announce each new video immediately after you publish it on YouTube.

Pro tip: Did you know that you can schedule posts in advance on social media sites and Hootsuite? Up your organizational game by scheduling YouTube videos and their respective social media blasts to be released around the same time.

Now for some technical tips for posting across different social media platforms. You must know how your content appears when you upload it to each website or app. To look as professional as possible, you don't want to have any images or videos cut off.

A video's aspect ratio describes the dimensions of the shape you're working with. In this case, your video is a rectangle, so the dimensions are abbreviated as long side to short side, or horizontal to vertical. If you use the wrong aspect ratio, information may be cut from your videos or images.

Here's the frustrating truth: different social media sites use different video aspect ratios. For example, Instagram is known for its square-shaped photos and videos, whereas YouTube videos are all wider than they are tall. YouTube's video player uses a 16:9 aspect ratio, which means the longer (horizontal) side is 16 inches and the shorter (vertical) side is nine.

You must know the aspect ratios of your social media platforms. At present, Facebook accepts both horizontally and vertically oriented videos. Instagram is in the same ballpark as Facebook, with the addition of square videos. Pinterest, on the other hand, uses square and vertical videos. LinkedIn and Twitter also have specific requirements.

The long and short of it is (geometry pun intended), you can repost your YouTube videos on all these social media sites, but you must work with the aspect ratios of each platform. To do this, you can resize images on your own, in Canva, or in other apps.

What To Post on Social Media

At a minimum, post the link to your YouTube video, and say a few words about it. Aim to incorporate some keywords in your description.

Also, post an image alongside your YouTube video link, especially the custom thumbnail you created for the video. Resize your image so that it's the right dimensions for the destination, whether it's Facebook, Instagram, or any others. Pay attention to aspect ratio to preserve your image. You can add a border, but don't let the image get cut off.

For extra credit, post a short portion of your video to give folks a teaser. Make it interesting, but don't give too much away. Your teaser should attract scrollers to click and see the whole video on YouTube, where they can also subscribe.

Finally, write up a short blurb for your social media blasts, and stir up some excitement for what you've just created. Down the line, you can offer subscriber incentives here. For example, offer a small incentive in return for subscribing to your channel. An incentive might be an additional video your audience has been asking for or a freebie like an eBook. Always include the link to your video and always ask people to subscribe.

Now, I (Lucas) have a confession to make. When I started my YouTube channel, I didn't do any blasts on my existing social media accounts. I started from scratch, using social media in… a different way.

After I got my channel up and running, I created new social media accounts whose branding matched my YouTube channel, with the same name and same logo. My channel ended up growing organically alongside my new social media accounts that were centered around the message of my channel.

This approach is an option for you. But you still want to share with the network you've already created on social media. This is an easy tactic to attract your first subscribers. When you're starting out, promote every video on all your active platforms. People already in your network want to support you.

After your first month or so, you can create new social media accounts whose branding matches your YouTube channel. Match the names and visual design, and post to these platforms every time you publish a new video on your channel.

Creating new social media accounts that promote your YouTube brand is a commitment. If you go this route, be sure to keep up with regular posting, and stay engaged by responding to comments on each platform. Finally, think about preserving the message of your YouTube channel. These new accounts are a part of your overall brand. So be consistent in what you say and how you communicate it.

Paid Advertising on Social Media

We don't recommend paid advertising until your channel is established and already has an organic following. You must understand your target audience and their interests before spending money to reach new people.

The exception is if your channel is an extension of an existing business. If you're clear on your message and have an advertising budget, you may consider running ads on Facebook, Instagram, Pinterest, etc.

If you're planning a big subscriber incentive, channel project announcement, or other channel-related news blast, you can use paid advertising to promote these initiatives and direct people back to your channel.

When setting up paid advertising, keep your ideal audience in mind. Whom do you want to reach with the ad? Who is actively looking for what you are offering or sharing? Most advertising platforms ask you to define who will see your ad. You can specify their location, age, gender, interests, and more. The most successful campaigns zero in on the perfect target audience. Don't waste your advertising dollars by casting your net too wide.

And if you're on a budget or still honing your message, hold onto your cash. You can post on social media for free and explore other marketing methods, like sharing with an email list.

Share With Your Email List

If you have an email list, send some newsletters to promote your channel launch. This is another opportunity to gain new subscribers from your existing network. Build excitement before and after you launch your new channel. Let people know why they should watch your videos and subscribe to your channel. And once your channel is live, keep sharing new videos with your subscribers.

You can also create YouTube videos to provide video marketing for your business. When you use YouTube to promote your business, your videos are the face of your marketing strategy. We talk more about video marketing below.

When you use email to direct people to YouTube, include an image from your video to break up paragraphs of text. Also, build up suspense or pose a question. Draw people into watching your YouTube video to find answers. You can give your readers a teaser of the video using a screenshot or thumbnail image within the body of the email. And of course, guide the reader to click the link that takes them to your video.

Another strategy is to use your email list to incentivize subscriptions to your channel. Or you can ask people one-on-one to subscribe to your channel when the opportunity arises. Chances are that folks want to hear from you and want to see what you're up to on YouTube. Subscribing to your channel costs them nothing but a minute, and then they'll be the first to know when you publish new content.

Video Marketing To Promote Your Channel and Business

When you share YouTube videos with an email list and ask for subscribers, you're not just promoting your channel. You're also using the intimacy of video marketing to help your clients get to know you, enhancing your brand.

As a business owner, consider embedding your YouTube videos on your website or in individual blog posts. You can also embed

YouTube videos in sales pages. Wherever customers go to buy something or learn about your product, use a video to create more engagement.

Pro tip: When you're in the YouTube Studio, there's a box that says "Allow Embed." Check this box so that your videos can be embedded on external websites.

Video marketing increases trust and helps potential customers learn more about you. The fact that you can house those videos on YouTube free of charge — and get paid for them once you are monetized — is an additional benefit.

Using videos to promote your brand helps grow your YouTube channel, which in turn promotes your brand. It's an effective circle. No matter where you embed your videos, your channel views and watch time increase, leading you towards monetization. Whether you promote on YouTube, your website, your blog, your landing pages, or on social media, your brand grows.

Step Four Summary

Here's a summary of what we covered:

- Launch your channel and encourage YouTube channel subscriptions with the help of your existing social media following and email list.
- Promote every video you post on existing social media channels. Use tools like Hootsuite to maximize time online, and schedule videos in advance.
- Consider creating social media accounts that are branded with your YouTube channel. Always keep up with those social media accounts, and post and comment frequently.
- Share your videos with your email list and draw people back to your YouTube channel.
- Ask for subscriptions one-on-one, whether over email, on social media, or even in person.

- When you promote your YouTube channel, you grow your channel *and* your business.

Action Steps

1. Make a list of all the places you can announce your channel, from social media to newsletters.

2. Share your first video in each of those places. Be sure to customize your posts for each platform. And remember to ask people to subscribe to your channel.

* * *

Next, we dive deeper into gaining your first 100 subscribers. We've already talked about creating quality videos, optimizing for SEO, and promoting your channel on social media. All these things help grow your following. But you can do better. In the next chapter, we share our two favorite strategies to accelerate your YouTube success.

8

GAIN YOUR FIRST 100 SUBSCRIBERS (STEP FIVE)

We've already discussed the value of social media and email lists in promoting your channel and becoming known. But how do people outside your network find you? In this chapter we answer that question.

We show you how to gain new subscribers by staying within the YouTube platform. We focus on two methods to build your subscriber list: responding to comments on your channel and connecting with other channels. We also discuss how to comment and why building a community on YouTube is necessary for your YouTube success.

Finally, we wrap up this section by emphasizing the qualities you need to be successful on YouTube.

Your goal is to gain your first 100 subscribers. But the truth is, your subscriber list probably won't go from zero to 100 overnight. Good things take time. And there are many factors here, including the size of your existing network and the amount of time you commit to YouTube.

But by staying consistent, you will reach that 100-subscriber mark and beyond. It all begins with understanding the YouTube community, what you have to offer, and how the community can benefit you.

Respond To Comments

If you want to build your subscriber list, you must respond to every comment on your channel. This is where the human connection comes in. Yes, there's a lot of automation, spam, and garbage in YouTubeland. But you can be a force for good!

Every person who leaves a comment or question on one of your videos is someone who took the time to view your content. Respond in an authentic and thoughtful way. And remember that interacting may be filling a void in someone's life. You never know when your response will make a real difference to someone else.

Engaging with people shows them that you want to build connections and help people. It's the whole "know, trust, and like" factor that's required in this digital age. Interact with your audience, and they will stay with you over the long term.

Responding to comments also shows prospective subscribers that there's a human behind the channel. You're not there to make a fast buck or solely for personal gain. In a time when people hide behind keyboards and human connection is hard to come by, this helps you build a reputation as a genuine person who cares about their audience.

Connect With Other Channels

Commenting on other channels is another way to connect with the YouTube community and gain subscribers. When you leave a comment, show that you watched the whole video by saying something specific to their channel or video. This makes you stand out from the crowd. It's much more effective than generic comments, like "Great video!", which many people post, all too often.

Directed comments help you build an audience, since they show other channels that you're supporting them. Make it a goal to connect with 20 channels within your niche. Look for channels with a sizable audience — i.e., a good number of subscribers — and watch and comment on their last 10 videos. Interacting through comments with popular YouTubers increases your own visibility. Doing this consistently builds your credibility and your subscriber list.

When so many videos on YouTube have millions of views, you may be wondering what a "good number" of subscribers is. Start with channels that have 1,000 to 5,000 subscribers (medium) or 5,000 to 15,000 subscribers (medium-large). Channels with over 30,000 subscribers are on a different level, and those with over 100,000 are big channels.

You can also connect with smaller channels (i.e., anything under 1,000 subscribers). This is still beneficial. Smaller channels often respond right away, and it's an opportunity to grow together. While you won't immediately gain the same number of connections, any visibility can serve you well.

On the other hand, aiming high can pay off. When I (Lucas) started out, I connected with a channel that had over 1 million subscribers. I commented on every video for several weeks. At first, I didn't receive any response, but I kept watching and commenting. And then, the surprise: this channel responded to me. I had shown that I was a regular supporter, not just a flyby.

This process creates new business opportunities with much bigger channels. Along with the connection to a successful YouTuber, you gain exposure to their subscribers. When people notice the conversation you're having in the comments, they might click through and check out your channel.

While you're connecting with other channels, don't forget to comment on comments. This is an effective method to gain the YouTuber's attention. Each time you comment on a comment, the channel owner receives a notification. Aside from the interaction with the commenter, this gets your name out there with popular channels.

The other channels within your niche are, technically, your competition. But have you ever heard the phrase "a rising tide lifts all boats"? When one channel in a niche becomes popular, the entire niche benefits. The whole community grows together. This is why you should think of your "competition" as "collaboration."

One final word of caution: while you're connecting with other channels in your niche, avoid going down the rabbit hole. Stay focused on your goals and be intentional with the time you spend on YouTube. Leaving ten detailed comments is more valuable than 50 generic comments. Also note the size of the channel you're interacting with. If you pursue connections with larger channels, make it part of a strategy, not a one-off decision.

Join Live Streams

Another method to boost your subscriber list is by joining live streams on YouTube. When you join a YouTube live stream, you connect with other channels, gain community, and increase visibility. On the other side, holding a live stream helps the host channel connect with their audience on a personal level.

My (Lucas's) early experience with YouTube live streams showed me the kind of connections that can happen on YouTube. Within the vastness of the internet, it's touching to find a group of people who share your interests and want to support you.

When my channel had just surpassed 100 subscribers, a stranger emailed me. He found my contact details on my channel's About page. He was also a YouTuber in my niche, and he invited me to join an upcoming live stream hosted by a larger channel.

After joining that live stream, my channel gained 50 new subscribers. That person saw the importance of this connection for me. Undoubtedly, he'd had a similar experience and knew how joining this live stream would grow my channel.

Research channels in your niche and find out when they go live. Then, tune in. After you join, don't just watch. Add comments, ask questions, and engage with other viewers in the chat window. Live streams are an opportunity to engage with the other channels who are watching, too. Look them up, get to know them, and connect.

Finally, while you watch... take notes on the host channel's live stream. Think: *What's working here? What would I want to do differently in my own live stream?* Because starting your own live stream is the next step.

Live Streaming: Your Turn

You can jump into live streaming at any point, regardless of how many subscribers you have. The key (as always) is consistency. Pick a schedule to go live and stick with it. Don't be deterred if you only have a handful of viewers to begin with.

When you are live, engage with viewers just like you would on other people's live streams. Respond to comments verbally and keep the conversation going.

Starting your own live streams can be intimidating to begin with. But it gets easier the more you do it. Plan out each live stream in advance. Center it around a common question, an event, a game, an interview, or another video type that works for you. Whatever you do, take advantage of the "live" element, and interact with your guests.

Tip: To host a live stream via mobile, you need to have at least 1,000 subscribers, whereas on your computer, there are no restrictions. Also, when you go live on your computer, you can use any type of computer camera, webcam, or DSLR camera (connected to your computer).

When you finish each live stream, the live video remains public on YouTube.

The Key To YouTube Success

Let's take a minute to step back and review. What makes for a successful YouTube channel? We know there are a lot of elements to remember, so let's recenter.

It's tempting to focus on the steps you need to take. And while you need a strategy, there's something else that's far more important. If you want to succeed in YouTube, you must:

1. Create a schedule.

2. Stick with it.

We've already discussed your editorial calendar. You must also plan out your promotional activities. Then, follow through and do the tasks you said you would. It's easy to start strong and then give up. Many people go all out, working 12-hour days, followed by complete burnout. We're advocating for the middle route. Set up a schedule that feels achievable, and then create the habit of honoring your calendar. If you can't commit to doing everything at once, just select a few essential tasks to focus on. Then, add more as you are able to commit more time.

Also, remember your reasons for starting your channel. Keep your goal and purpose in mind, especially when the going gets tough. Monetization is a great goal when starting out. Before you can monetize your channel, you need 1,000 subscribers and 4,000 watch hours. This unlocks access to multiple forms of revenue and keeps you motivated through the early days. We discuss monetization in the next chapter.

Here's a reminder of the items you should already have added to your editorial calendar:

- Videos: a plan for the creation and frequency of your posts. Include the time of day when each video will go live.
- Social media blasts: a schedule for promoting your videos after you've published them.

- Newsletters: when you will promote your videos via email or send newsletters for other marketing purposes.

Now here are more tasks to include, along with suggestions for a consistent schedule:

- Brainstorm new content. Do this at least once a month (depending on your video schedule).
- Research relevant and low-competition keywords and tags. Do this at least quarterly.
- Respond to comments on your channel. Two or three times a week.
- Connect with other channels through commenting. Several times a week.
- Connect with other channels by joining live streams. At least twice a month.
- Plan your own live streams and go live. One regular time, once a week.

Finally, remember to set new goals once you've achieved the smaller landmarks. After you reach 100 subscribers, aim for 250 and so on.

Step Five Summary

To gain your first 100 subscribers, you must be a responsive voice on your own channel. Here's a recap of step five:

- Reply to every comment that people post on your videos. Be human, and be kind.
- Set a goal to connect with 20 channels in your own niche. By commenting on their videos and joining their live streams, you'll get noticed.
- Be consistent. Create a schedule of tasks and stick with it.

Action Steps

1. Set up your editorial calendar in Trello or a similar app that combines a calendar and a to-do list. Include a weekly plan for the creation of your video content and your goals for regular publishing.

2. Set aside "connecting" time in your calendar several times per week. This time will be spent commenting on 20 channels in your niche, responding to comments on your own channel, and joining live streams.

* * *

Rinse and repeat these steps until you reach your goals, including the required subscribership and watch hours for monetization. Next up, we explore how to make money on YouTube as well as what you should expect when you arrive.

We also share our favorite YouTube success stories. These people all built their channels from the ground up and now have thriving businesses on YouTube. They provide insider tips and answer the question, "What do you wish you had known at the beginning of your YouTube journey?"

9

MONETIZE YOUR CHANNEL (STEP SIX)

So far we've discussed how to attract people to your YouTube channel through consistently making great content, promoting yourself across your network, and connecting with other channels in your niche. By applying the first five steps, your channel will grow to 100, then 200, and eventually 1,000 subscribers.

But what happens when you reach 1,000 subscribers? Because yes, with persistence, you will get there. This is a key milestone because it's when you can monetize your YouTube channel. In this chapter we discuss everything you need to know about monetization so that you can maximize your YouTube income.

Monetization is the primary way people make money on YouTube. It involves joining the YouTube Partner Program, then earning money through various methods. In order to apply for the YouTube Partner Program, you must meet the subscriber and watch hour requirements. They are:

- 1,000 subscribers, and
- 4,000 watch hours over the last 12 months.

Up to this point, we've focused on gaining subscribers. But what are "watch hours," and why does YouTube make this a requirement for monetization?

Watch hours are important because they show the total amount of time people have spent viewing your videos. Watch time is the best indicator to see if your content is engaging viewers. If there are any "empty promises" on your channel (like misleading titles or tags, or low-quality content), viewers find that out very quickly. Potential subscribers who've been burned won't come back.

You must attract viewers who are passionate about the type of content you provide. These are the people who support you on a personal level and not because you've swapped subscribers, i.e., "I'll subscribe to your channel if you subscribe to mine." Organic engagement from people who love your videos is key to your success on YouTube. This is why watch time is a key metric.

All your statistics, including subscribers and watch hours, can be found in your channel's Analytics page. Your analytics are an essential part of your YouTube process. You can use them to set future goals for your channel based on your current numbers. We cover how to analyze your data for maximum growth in Chapter Eleven.

When you apply for the YouTube Partner Program, you must wait for approval. YouTube approves channels that meet their community guidelines and the watch time and subscriber requirements. YouTube holds regular channel reviews to verify that their Partners continue to follow the community guidelines. If you're making family-friendly content, you shouldn't encounter any problems.

After you get approved, you set up a Google AdSense account (to receive payment from ad revenue) and a direct deposit so you can get paid in a timely fashion.

Once you're approved for monetization, here are four opportunities to make money on YouTube. Note that YouTube has specific eligibility requirements for each method, although there's some overlap between them.

1. Ad Revenue

We all know what it's like to sit through an ad while we're waiting for a YouTube video to start playing. While ad revenue is the most well-known way to monetize your channel, it isn't your only option.

Note: YouTube Premium account holders pay to not see ads when watching YouTube videos. However, you still earn money from YouTube Premium users. YouTube shares their monthly membership fee with you. Best of all, the more videos they watch, the more money you make.

2. Channel Memberships

In channel memberships, subscribers pay you a monthly recurring fee to access your content and receive monthly perks. You can offer a variety of member-only perks, including badges, emojis, personalized videos, member-only live chats, and more.

3. Super Chat

When you go live on YouTube, viewers can send a Super Chat (an amount of money) to support you. Super Chats are highlighted in the chat, so they are seen by other channels who are watching. The donator supports you while gaining visibility. In order to receive this income, be sure to select "Accept Super Chats" when you're setting up for monetization.

4. Merchandising

Larger channels can take advantage of "merch shelves" within YouTube. This is where you showcase your branded merchandise with your channel's designs. You need an account with a merchandise retailer, such as Teespring, which you then integrate with YouTube. You can sell coffee cups, pillows, sweatshirts, and more through YouTube, and your channel keeps the revenue.

For smaller channels, you can also sell merchandise or other products without YouTube's third-party assistance. For example, for arts and crafts, you could link sales pages to your YouTube channel, or sell your products on live streams or in a "live auction" setting. This is another way to use YouTube's marketing platform to gain visibility and receive direct revenue from the sale of your products.

Getting Approved for Monetization

So now that we've painted the picture of what monetization can offer you, how do you get there? Start by setting a goal of hitting the watch time and subscriber benchmarks needed to apply for monetization. We recommend aiming to reach these levels within one year. If you commit more time to growing your channel, you can get there sooner.

Once you submit your application, YouTube sends you an email receipt. Then, their team members review your channel and watch your videos to verify that you're following the rules. For family-friendly content, you should receive approval without any problems. Channels about restricted topics, such as gun tutorials, may find it harder to get approved. They must follow YouTube's guidelines to a T.

In either case, be patient. The approval process takes anywhere from two weeks to four and a half months. It depends on how busy Google is, as their team members are manually reviewing your channel. Once approved, your channel becomes eligible to earn ad revenue and other forms of income.

What To Expect From Monetization

You may be wondering how much money you can make on YouTube. In this section we explore some realistic numbers when starting out, with examples from ad revenue and Super Chat. Later in this chapter, we share three case studies from more established YouTubers.

We're not gonna lie: ad revenue can be disappointing. Smaller channels can expect to earn pennies at first. It's best to view ad revenue as a secondary benefit and not the primary reason for creating a YouTube channel. Instead, focus on using YouTube as free marketing for your business and take advantage of the other monetization methods.

Having said that, even if your channel is small, it's still worth enabling ad revenue. Set yourself up for success in the future. As your following grows, so does your income from ads. The more time people spend watching your videos, i.e., your watch time, the greater your ad revenue. And this income is entirely passive once your videos are published.

Super Chat offers higher income potential for newer channels, especially if you have an engaged audience who wants to support you. To give you a sense of what you can earn on Super Chat, here are some numbers from my (Lucas's) live streams about fishing. Individual payments range from $1 all the way up to $100… it can be exciting, as you never know what you might earn. Be aware that YouTube takes a 30% cut off Super Chat income.

Losing Monetization Status

When you achieve monetization, you can't sit back and rest on your laurels. Monetization is just the first stage in growing your following — and income — on YouTube.

While breaks are sometimes necessary, we recommend maintaining a consistent presence at least until you are well established and have a reliable monthly income. If you're inactive on your channel for six months, you could fall below the watch time threshold of 4,000 hours in 12 months. If you drop below this threshold, YouTube may remove you from the Partner Program.

If you are demonetized, you can appeal the decision. YouTube gives you specific information on why it happened and how to fix the issue. You can then make the necessary adjustments to your channel and reapply for monetization status.

Case Study #1

We sat down with a group of successful YouTubers, each in a different niche, to hear about their experience. All these folks built their channels from the ground up. They were persistent and applied for monetization as soon as they were eligible.

YouTube has provided these people with the opportunity to expand their brands and fuel their passions and hobbies. In these short interviews, they share the reasons behind their success.

First, we meet Allison Lindstrom. Besides her thriving YouTube channel, Allison runs a successful blogging business. She started her channel when her blogging business was just over a year old. Allison saw how video would help humanize her brand.

Channel name: Allison Lindstrom

Niche: How to run a blogging business

Audience: Busy stay-at-home moms

Channel stats (as of summer 2020):

- 57,000+ subscribers
- 2.6+ million all-time views and 60,000+ watch hours

First public video: Published in September 2016

How did you decide on your niche?

I've always been passionate about running a business from home. Initially I blogged about various categories. But as my site grew, I started to figure out what was working (and what wasn't). So I shared my findings with readers. They responded well, and I began to focus on the home-business-and-blogging niche. My YouTube channel is an extension of my blog. I make videos on the same topics that I write about.

How long did it take you to monetize?

I published my first YouTube video on September 15, 2016. I received my first check from YouTube in June 2017. It was for $191.54 .

I could have monetized sooner. But when I signed up for Google Ads and started posting videos, I forgot to enter my bank information, so they didn't know where to send my ad money. Rookie mistake!

In my first nine months, before receiving that initial check, I posted 45 videos on YouTube. That's an average of five videos per month, which is more than one video per week. I think this volume and consistency helped me gain visibility on YouTube.

What strategies worked for you to get your first 100 subscribers?

The first strategy is using applicable keywords to describe each video I posted. This helps with SEO.

The second is posting consistently for an entire year. People don't want to subscribe to a channel that only has five videos. By posting new content often, you show viewers that you are here to stay. This helps you build a loyal following who tune in each week to view your latest content.

What was the hardest part about getting started?

The hardest part for me was getting comfortable in front of the camera; also, finding an efficient editing process. My first videos are so cringe-worthy — I'm obviously not at ease. But the only option was to keep posting. I'm so glad I did because now I can record a video at any time with no problem.

What's the hardest part now?

Nowadays I struggle with responding to everyone's comments and scheduling my videos far enough in advance. I dream of getting six months ahead one day. But these are wonderful problems to have. My consistent hard work has paid off.

What are you doing for marketing right now?

I share my videos with my email list, on my Pinterest account, and in my private Facebook groups. When I'm promoting a specific business project or subscriber incentive, I occasionally use Facebook ads as well.

Most of my views come from organic traffic when people search for a keyword I have targeted. I know that most of my followers either go to Google or YouTube when searching for something. So I look at YouTube the same way I look at Google, and use as many descriptive, SEO-rich keywords as possible.

Do you do everything yourself when it comes to your channel? If not, what do you hire out?

I currently do 100% of the work on my channel; however, I outsource a lot of my blogging tasks. If I didn't hire people to help me with that portion of my business, I wouldn't have enough time to handle my YouTube channel. I enjoy the video aspect of my business, so this is one thing I keep doing. It helps that I now have an efficient process to create, upload, and share my videos.

Do you have any final words of wisdom?

Try to create videos that have a unique perspective or spin on them. Videos like "Top Five ____ to ____" are great, but people love it even more when you think outside the box.

I post a combination of creative videos (like "Top Five Blog Niche Ideas My 3,000+ Blogging Students Choose") and evergreen videos (like "How to Write a Blog Post for Beginners").

Every piece of content should teach something or inspire someone. "Life update" videos are fun to see occasionally, but focus on creating fresh value 99.99% of the time.

Case Study #2

The next interview features an entirely different niche: scratch-off lottery tickets. Ondrei, the creator of "Get Rich or Die Scratching," chose this niche because he wanted to make videos without showing his face. Later, he became more comfortable on camera.

Even though this niche has little in common with the blogging sphere, many of the factors that contributed to Ondrei's success are similar to Allison's story.

Channel name: "Get Rich or Die Scratching"

Niche: Scratch-off lottery tickets

Channel stats (as of August 2020):

- 16k+ subscribers
- 2.7 million views and 224k+ watch hours

Channel started: March 2019

How long did it take you to monetize your channel?

I monetized two days shy of two months after starting my channel.

What are you doing for marketing right now?

I rely on the YouTube algorithm and always incorporate SEO-optimized keywords in my videos. I have no other social media or marketing in place, yet I just added over 2,000 subscribers in one month.

What was the hardest part about getting started?

My channel is about lottery tickets, so there is some financial overhead. The hardest part for me was budgeting for the cost of buying tickets. Having never gambled before, I was unprepared for this. I was close to giving up before I received approval for monetization. Monetization covered my costs and solved this problem!

What strategies worked for you to get your first 100 subscribers?

Posting videos consistently. Also, learning about custom thumbnails and SEO-rich video titles made a big difference. These two elements are so important for getting found on YouTube.

Finally, I got super lucky. About a month after I started my channel, I made a video on a new lottery ticket that came out the same day. That ticket became the best-selling ticket in Florida, and my video received a lot of views. I gained over 2,000 subscribers and generated over $3,500 in ad revenue from that one video. This helped get my channel off the ground.

Case Study #3

Finally, we step into yet another niche: a kids' channel. One of the creators of this channel, Katie, told us that she never intended to start a YouTube channel. Her son took the first step and became the heart of their channel. "Kids Adventures with Sweetie Fella Aleks" features several of the YouTube video types we have discussed, including toy reviews, family vlogs, and playing games.

Channel name: "Kids Adventures with Sweetie Fella Aleks"

Niche: Kids, young families

Channel stats (as of August 2020):

- 6.48k subscribers
- 2.3 million views and 79k watch hours

Channel started: September 2016

Why did you start your channel?

Our channel began when our son told me, "I want to make videos with toys." He has always been photogenic and is comfortable around the camera. Sweetie Fella Aleks just loves entertaining other people. We thought it would preserve family moments when we travel, and it would be fun to play with different toys and gadgets with our son. So we went for it.

What strategies worked for you to grow your subscriber list?

In the beginning we had no idea what to expect. The first 100 subscribers came fast, thanks to our networking with other channels who were producing similar content. We also recorded and posted our videos regularly. The growth from 100 to 1,000 took around two months.

What was the hardest part about getting started?

Finding out what our viewers want to see and what content could captivate our audience. In our niche, our audience is mainly kids. The challenge is greater, as kids can get bored easily. Kids also don't leave many comments, so it's hard to know what they like or don't like about your video. Sometimes it surprises you that a certain video has more watch time and views than others.

What's the hardest part now?

Uploading interesting content on a set schedule is the biggest day-to-day challenge. Being consistent is essential — viewers expect videos around the same day and time. It's a lot of work to make quality videos. You have to record, edit, describe, code, etc. This takes more time than some people realize.

For example, a three-minute video takes us up to two hours of editing, an hour to make a thumbnail and description, and another 30 minutes to finalize the process and post the video on YouTube.

Do you have any final words of wisdom?

Natural growth is essential because it brings steady watch time. If individuals are not subscribing because of real interest in your videos, they aren't likely to stay around to watch them. The result: your watch time is low.

Getting to understand YouTube and how the algorithm codes videos is also essential. But the best part of making family videos is that you spend time with your kids and have fun together.

Step Six Summary

You made it to the end of the final step. Here's a summary of what we covered in this chapter:

- Monetization means being approved to join the YouTube Partner Program and making money on YouTube.
- Make it a goal to reach the requirements for monetization eligibility within one year.
- After you monetize, continue to grow your channel. Be sure to keep your watch time above the 4,000-hour threshold.
- There are many opportunities to make money on YouTube besides ad revenue, including marketing your business, Super Chat, channel memberships, and merchandising.

There's a place for you on YouTube. Monetization is just the beginning.

In the case studies, we saw how the magic happens after monetization. How will your channel open up your business? What kind of marketing will you use? The possibilities, and the means of interaction with your new or existing brand, are endless.

We hope that some of these YouTube perspectives showed you that any niche can see success on YouTube. If you create content that you're passionate about, and if you're consistent and stick with it, you will find a loyal audience and an income on YouTube.

Action Steps

1. Take a minute to write down the "Why" behind your YouTube channel. Is there anything personal to you about your niche or your target audience? Write it down. Remind yourself what this is all about for you.

2. Reflect on how monetization would help you reach your YouTube goals.

* * *

We have covered the six steps to start and monetize a YouTube channel. But we're not finished yet! Next, we dig into yet another method to make money with your new YouTube skills. We show you how to cash in as a freelance YouTube Content Strategist.

10

OFFER YOUTUBE MARKETING SERVICES

Whether you're on your way to monetizing your channel or whether you've arrived, there are more opportunities to profit from your YouTube skills. In this chapter we delve into making money from YouTube by offering your skills to other business owners.

As a beginner YouTuber, you probably expected that the primary way to make money is from your own YouTube channel. While monetization is an excellent goal, we're all for adding side hustles that leverage the skills you've gained in your personal projects or brand-building on YouTube.

If you're taking the leap into freelancing, looking to change careers, or seeking to learn from other business owners, you can create additional income by offering YouTube marketing services. The B2B (business to business) freelance possibilities are endless.

Since you've already put the effort into mastering YouTube, why not use your skills to add another revenue stream while you grow your channel?

YouTube boasts billions of users, and savvy business owners can take advantage of the platform to grow their brand and business. The more fluent and efficient they are on the platform, the more success and visibility their marketing has. Yet many business owners either do not have the time or lack the knowledge to make the most of this opportunity. That is where you come in.

The Content Marketing Bonanza

Content marketing is perfect for YouTube, and YouTube is perfect for content marketing.

Content marketing differs from product marketing in that it isn't about pushing specific products or services. Instead, it's about offering experiences for your audience to engage with your brand. The goal is not to "sell" anything. Rather, it's a chance for your audience to find out more about you and your business, and it builds brand loyalty.

So why is YouTube perfect for content marketing, and vice versa?

Well, YouTube has the potential to showcase any element of your business, whether you're providing education, entertainment, or other evidence of the uniqueness of your brand. Video offers a window into your personality, your humanness. The possibilities for fans to connect with you on YouTube and engage with your content are limitless.

In recent years, online content marketing has exploded in popularity, from blogs to podcasts to video. Any business that isn't currently using YouTube is missing out on this user-friendly — and free — content marketing experience. As a virtual service provider, your YouTube marketing services can help take your client's business to that next level: using the medium of video to grow and engage their audience.

Types of Clients

So now that you've developed a list of enviable YouTube skills, it's time to call them what they are: video marketing skills. The next step is pitching your skills to potential clients. There are many different types of clients, but not all clients are created equal. Let's explore the different types so that you know whom to pitch and whom to avoid.

The first possibility is the individual who isn't currently on YouTube. They want to get monetized for a channel they haven't yet started.

Pass! This person doesn't have a budget, and they don't have any revenue coming in. Even though it's a low-cost venture for most businesses to start a YouTube channel, you still deserve to get paid.

The second option is the individual with an established YouTube channel that's already monetized. They want to scale their channel and income. They're hiring an assistant or remote service provider to free up their own time.

Because they've been around for a while, this person has an established profit history. They know how they spend their time (and how they should be spending their time), what their effective hourly rate is, and what they can afford to pay somebody to perform tasks they should no longer be doing.

Go for it! There's no better place to profit and grow than by working with an established channel.

The final client is the profitable business who isn't using YouTube effectively (or at all). They need help implementing a YouTube strategy to market their business.

This person is missing out — send them your pitch!

However, don't pitch to any business or client with zero or limited YouTube presence. Instead, look for healthy businesses who aren't yet taking advantage of all that YouTube has to offer. When you're seeking businesses to pitch, research their YouTube presence (if any). Find out how their business is doing in general. What products or services do they offer? How big is their following on other platforms?

You also want to pitch to businesses or industries that interest you. If you care about the subject matter, even better. Look for potential clients who can offer a positive working relationship in which both of you can grow.

Five YouTube Marketing Services

When you pitch a client, have confidence in your skills and experience as a YouTube Marketing Specialist. Below are five valuable YouTube marketing skills you can offer other businesses.

But remember: actions speak louder than words. As you go through these five service offerings, practice them on your own channel first. Once you have results, your YouTube experience will be more convincing to that first, second, and third client. And as your experience grows, you can charge more for getting results.

1. Video Editing and Graphic Design

For technical setup, understand the equipment a client needs, lighting requirements, and non-distracting video backgrounds. Some graphic design knowledge is also handy when it comes to creating and sizing channel banner art, thumbnails, and video end screens.

If graphic design or video editing sparks a passion, then dive deep. There's room for creativity here that clients need. After learning the basics, you can get fancy designing, animating, and editing video content.

Video editing is an easy way to get your foot in the door with a new client. There are numerous businesses who need one-off videos edited. You can offer your services on a project basis. Then, once you've established your expertise, talk to clients about their other video marketing needs. Let them know how you can help them use YouTube for their business. Clients who have a good experience with you may want to keep you on retainer for their future video needs.

2. Channel Setup and Optimization

For a client who doesn't have an established YouTube presence, you can get their YouTube account up and running smoothly with the goal of reaching 100 subscribers as soon as possible.

Chapter Eight walks through the best strategies to reach 100 subscribers. Or, for a complete list of tactics, check out our free guide, "10 Steps to Your First 100 YouTube Subscribers," that you can download here: **uploaduniversity.com/book-bonus/**

Existing YouTube channels can benefit from a full review. You can list out all the things you'd do to optimize the client's channel. This might include niching down, graphic design, thumbnails, video titles, and SEO. You may also want to write a fresh About page and ensure that their keywords are still relevant to their content.

3. Managing the Content Schedule (Editorial Calendar)

One useful skill you can offer clients is managing their editorial calendar. Help them plan out what content is released and when. Creating an editorial calendar keeps you organized and is the best way to ensure that your client posts consistently.

As you brainstorm video content ideas, discuss the following with your client:

- What's the theme or goal of the channel?
- What's their niche? What are their relevant subcategories?

From here, you can suggest new video ideas and add them to the calendar. You can also come up with new video ideas using a keyword generator and find search terms that are popular but not competitive. Focus on the needs and questions of your client's customers and use relevant keywords for their audience. We discussed how to find keywords and create an editorial calendar in Chapter Four.

When creating an editorial calendar with a client, take time to discuss the following:

- How often is it realistic for the client's channel to post regularly? You must both commit to the same posting schedule.

- How much time can you and your client devote to making new videos?

Each client has a different editorial calendar. The goal is manageability and consistency, not burnout. Make a schedule that fits your time, your client's time, and your client's budget.

This calendar management role can also extend to encompass other project management tasks, if needed. The project manager's main role is to keep things on track. If you have strong organizational skills, you will quickly become an asset to your client. Meanwhile, your client (the "big picture" person) gives you the tools you need to get your job done.

4. Comment Moderation

Maintaining a regular presence on your client's channel is imperative to your client's customer service. While it isn't a traditional customer service role, commenting is the most consistent human-to-human interaction of your client's brand with their YouTube audience.

Comment moderation involves responding to all comments posted on your client's videos. Don't forget to also follow up on comments to comments. As always with YouTube and with customer service, be human, and be kind.

Also keep your client's goals in mind. Are they more focused on subscriber growth or making new connections on YouTube? If connections are important, pay attention to comments left by other channels within your client's niche. Visit their channel and take time to comment on their videos. Help your client build new connections on YouTube. For more details about commenting, review Chapter Eight.

5. Keyword Research

Don't skip over keywords and tags. If you don't use them, your client's videos won't appear in search results. Every quarter, review your client's analytics and look at keywords related to their niche. When you begin with a new client, you want to do that work right away. We cover YouTube analytics in the next chapter.

There's plenty of free software that analyzes and generates keywords for you. Once you have a list of relevant keywords for your client's channel, ensure their natural placement in video titles, video descriptions, tags, and channel tags.

Technical note: A channel administrator (i.e., the content owner) can invite team members to help manage their videos and content. This is how a client can give you access to their channel.

Return on Investment (ROI)

As a YouTube Marketing Specialist, you must show your clients how your work provides them with a positive return on investment (ROI). When a client hires you, they want to see results: more website traffic, increased subscriber counts, larger number of views, and increased revenue. Understanding the complex landscape of social media marketing can help you set expectations with your client about their ROI.

The first thing you need to know is your client's goal. If your client's goal is monetization, they need to be patient. Growing enough watch hours to reach monetization is a slow and steady build. If they're hiring you to monetize a new channel and are paying you for ten hours of work per week for 12 months, they might not see a return on investment for more than six months. That's why you should work with a client who has reasonable expectations.

It's not always possible to calculate an exact ROI from every marketing activity. Without a bunch of fancy tools, there's no way to establish which conversion is attributed to which social media platform. And even with such tools, you won't have the full picture.

Ultimately, all the elements of a marketing strategy work together to move somebody through the customer life cycle, from unaware of your business, to subscriber, and eventually to paying (and hopefully repeat) customer.

While you're thinking about your client's ROI, also ask the question: *How else can we use this content?*

Your client can use the videos you create for them outside of YouTube. It's a no-brainer to create short videos featuring your client's company, showing people "here's what it's like to work with us." These videos can then be featured on the client's website, sales and landing pages, and other social media sites.

Finally, be versatile in your service offerings. Pitching short-term projects helps get clients on board who don't want to commit to a larger YouTube marketing budget. For instance, you can produce enough video content to showcase their business, on a project-based timeline, for a one- or three-month engagement.

This condensed project structure is still valuable. A client can go from an empty channel to having a collection of stunning videos that show people how they do their work. Then, further emphasize the value of your work by showing a client how they can reuse the videos on their website and other social media platforms.

From Service Provider To YouTube Content Strategist

When starting out, look for clients who already have a YouTube channel with established systems and processes. When you step in to help with their channel, you'll know more about YouTube than the average virtual service provider and can take tasks off their plate, while also learning from your client and developing your skills. It's a win-win!

Working with clients who already have their channels up and running gives you insight into a thriving YouTube channel. As you work with more clients and gain familiarity with different industries, you'll develop more specialized skills, which means you can take the leap into becoming a YouTube Content Strategist.

As a content strategist who is experienced with the ins and outs of YouTube marketing, you can charge for coaching, strategy, or consulting services. The deeper you specialize in YouTube marketing and the more you can show proof that your methods work, the more valuable you are to clients.

For businesses that want to start a YouTube channel from scratch, you can create a YouTube strategy for them that aligns with the goals of their business. And if they want to hire you to do the work to carry out that plan, then, awesome!

On the freelancing site Upwork, YouTube Video Editors charge around $25 per hour. YouTube Specialists and YouTube SEO Gurus, on the other hand, are charging $32-$125 per hour. Most freelancers with these specialized skills earn between $50-$100 per hour.

As you gain experience and credibility, consider styling yourself as a YouTube Content Strategist, Consultant, or Coach. Take yourself to that next level and increase your rates by diving deep and gaining experience in this coveted field.

Action Steps

1. Make a list of the industries or companies that most inspire you. Where could you see yourself doing YouTube marketing?

2. Continue brainstorming or do some research to create a list of five businesses you'd like to work with. Bonus step: send them a pitch!

* * *

Coming up next, we return our focus to your channel. We talk about your channel's long-term growth and walk through what you need to do to ensure your future YouTube success.

11

YOUTUBE SUCCESS

Joining the YouTube Partner Program is a highlight in your YouTube career. Congratulations! You just added a revenue arm to your business, brand, or hobby.

We've discussed the income-generating opportunities YouTube has to offer via the YouTube Partner Program, including ad revenue, channel memberships, Super Chat, and more. But arriving at monetization is only the first step in your YouTube journey. As your channel grows, you automatically receive more money from each of these revenue streams.

Long-term growth is the foundation of YouTube success. So how can you accelerate the growth of your channel... and your income?

The key is to keep creating engaging content and building your watch hours. You've already mastered the basics. Now keep to your posting schedule and show up consistently for your new audience. They will thank you for it — and so will your bank account.

While creating content, look for ways to improve each stage of the process, from producing videos to optimizing and revising your channel. In this chapter we explore some practical steps you can take to help your channel thrive. We discuss:

- How to read your analytics
- What to do if you're not getting views
- Ways to keep improving and adding to your channel

We start with the analytics page on your channel. It's essential you understand these numbers so that you can get better results on YouTube.

How To Read Your Analytics

You must get to know your analytics page in YouTube Studio. It shows subscriber count, watch hours, number of views, and more. Before monetization, you need to check your analytics for the eligibility requirements: 1,000 subscribers and 4,000 watch hours. After monetization, you will use these numbers to improve your channel.

When studying your analytics page, you are looking to see what has worked for your recent videos. Then, try to do more of what's working and less of what isn't. But don't make too many adjustments at once. When you do this, you won't know which changes are responsible for increasing your views.

How frequently should you check your analytics?

Analytics are a balance. You have to know what's happening, but don't let obsession over "likes" get in the way of your productivity. Keep your larger goals in mind and know that every channel starts slow.

For the first 90 days of your channel, check your analytics weekly. After that, a monthly review makes the most sense long-term.

What should you look for in your analytics?

Your analytics page displays a lot of data. Focus on the essentials and don't get overwhelmed. For example, the analytics page shows you:

- Watch time
- Views (over past X amount of time, i.e., weeks, months, etc.)

- View duration
- Watch time from subscribers
- Top videos
- Impressions ranking
- Click-through rate
- Traffic source type
- Ranking searches through Yahoo, Google, Facebook, etc.
- Top search terms
- And more!

For now, zero in on the three critical pieces of data to gauge your progress. They are:

- Total views
- Watch time (hours)
- Subscribers

Here's an example of how these look on my (Gina's) analytics page:

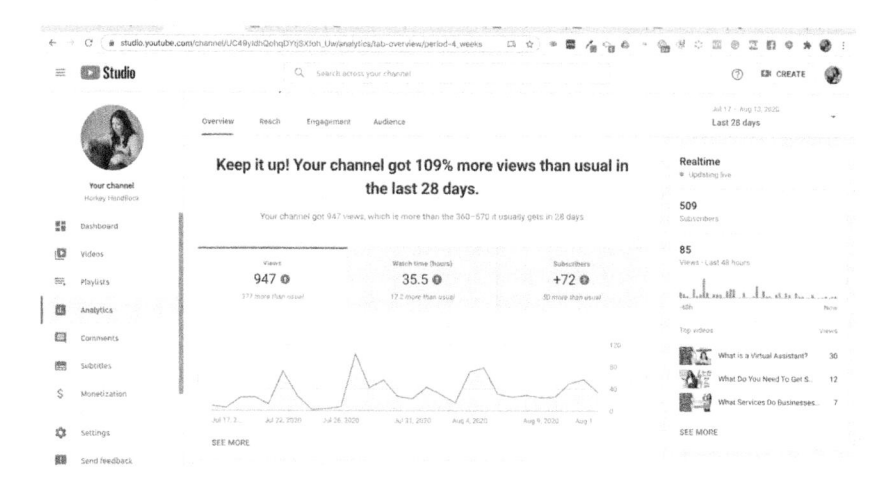

Total views starts low for most new channels. As your following grows, your views increase. You'll notice that you get the most views per day (aka daily views) on the first day you publish a video. Views are a "tortoise and the hare" situation. Slow and steady wins the race. Keep posting according to your schedule and you'll see a gradual upward trend over time.

Views can be a misleading number. They say less about your success than watch time. When someone watches at least 30 seconds of a video, that counts as one total "view," even if your video is seven minutes long, whereas watch time shows the total amount of time people spend actually watching your videos.

To judge how well you're retaining folks once they come to your channel, you need one more piece of data: audience retention.

Audience retention is the percentage of viewers who watch your video (or leave) over the course of the video. It's rare for people to watch an entire YouTube video; most leave immediately if they get bored. If a video achieves 50% audience retention (i.e., viewers, on average, watch half of that video), that's gold star status!

Pro tip: Within YouTube's Audience Retention Report, there's something called absolute retention. Absolute retention shows the precise moments in a video where viewers stop watching. It also displays the "most watched" moments. This allows you to further gauge what's working in your videos (and what's not).

The longer viewers spend watching your videos, the higher your total watch time. For monetization, you need to keep watch hours at 4,000 hours per 12 months. Utilize your audience retention to get into the perspective of your viewers: what kept them watching video X rather than video Y? As you analyze your viewer retention rate, you can increase successes across your channel as well as keep watch hours at their peak.

Sometimes your "evergreen content" videos won't appear popular in the beginning. Evergreen content is successful because the watch time climbs over time. The more content you have on the internet and the longer it soaks, the more it gains traction and visibility.

Sometimes an old video — that may not be your highest-quality video — unexpectedly gains a lot of views. This happens because as you post more content on YouTube, your success compounds. Newer videos give older videos a boost. So continue putting your energy into making more content.

When you have enough data, compare views and watch time across different video types. Reflect on what you did with one video versus another. This is how successful YouTubers figure out what is speaking to their audience.

Also, be aware that lower ratings have more to do with being new on YouTube, or sometimes they are just a fluke. Don't sweat the small stuff! For now, get used to your analytics, but don't obsess over them. And keep producing new content. The more consistent you are, the more success you have.

Finally, keep up with your subscriber count to see how near you are to your monetization goals. Analyzing your subscriber count over time can also tell you what's working (or not working) with your promotional efforts.

Note: When you review analytics, you can check month-by-month, quarter-by-quarter, and year-by-year figures to gauge your growth over time.

How To Get More Views

There's a lot of mystique around this, especially when it comes to making viral videos. But there are factors that you can control to produce successful videos and make money on YouTube.

I (Lucas) have been on YouTube for two years. And I've noticed that a video with a strong title, thumbnail, and description can become popular right away. Constantly optimizing these elements improves the visibility of your videos, no matter where you are in your YouTube journey. Chapter Six dealt with how to optimize these components of your videos.

Let's take a short dive into the YouTube algorithm, i.e., how video visibility is controlled by YouTube itself. You can influence the algorithm if you know how it works. For instance, if a sizable amount of people "like" a video in the first 10 minutes after uploading, YouTube's algorithm gives that video more visibility.

If a video appears to be shooting upwards in popularity, YouTube puts it on the "suggested videos" list for viewers who are watching similar content. When one of your videos is on the "suggested" or "recommended" videos list, more people are likely to watch it. Some channels have exploded in popularity in this way, by accident or on purpose.

Let's review what might adversely affect a video's success.

Note: YouTube takes 24-48 hours to show the most recent data on your videos. So don't obsess over numbers for content you just published.

If a video performs poorly, review the following components:

- Thumbnail: make sure it reads well, that the image is clear, and that the graphics and words are eye-catching.
- Video title: reread it and verify that it makes sense and accurately describes the video.
- Keywords: check that they are relevant to your video and not too difficult to rank for.
- Tags: use relevant tags and avoid tagging popular current events, as there's too much competition for those tags.

Also, double-check that the video has been published as "public." After you've reviewed these things, and especially if you're creating evergreen content, be patient. Most content doesn't shoot up in popularity, but it does grow steadily over time. The payoff comes later.

When a video performs well, repeat and maximize your success. Finally, remember your stats can be affected by many factors, including:

- Content strategy (what you're posting, your topics, the length of your videos)
- Posting frequency
- Time of year/seasonal trends
- Current events (e.g., COVID-19)
- Popularity of keywords
- Promotional efforts

Optimize Video Length

As you're optimizing your channel, consider adjusting your video length to increase your ad revenue. For your first videos, 3-5 minutes is a good benchmark. This helps you hone your ideas, especially if you're talking and trying to keep your videos succinct.

But don't rule out longer videos, as long as they provide compelling content. Videos that are 10-15 minutes in length receive a lot of views. And throughout 2019 and 2020, 25-minute videos rose in popularity. People are spending more time — formerly TV-watching time — on YouTube. As a platform, YouTube is becoming a big part of our entertainment experience.

As well as being popular, longer videos can maximize your ad revenue on YouTube. With longer videos, you can include more than one ad. We recommend placing ads at the end of a buildup, right before something exciting happens or some question is answered. This incentivizes viewers to keep watching your video after the ad.

The lesson is: don't get attached to short videos so that you can later take advantage of this extra income opportunity.

Keep Improving and Adding To Your Channel

Let's zoom out and take a big-picture view of your channel. For long-term growth, you must continuously improve and add to your channel. As you spend more time on the platform, you'll see what's working for other YouTubers and can incorporate those things into your own channel.

No matter how much experience you have on YouTube, here are some ways that your channel can continually improve:

Video Content and Production

When you become more comfortable making videos, you'll find that there's an infinite number of opportunities to improve your content. Take it one step at a time, whether that means refining your research or editing process, buying better-quality equipment, or posting more frequently.

The road to improving your content is a long one. Keep producing consistently, but be careful to avoid burnout.

Visual Design and Branding

There are many ways you can improve your designs, making them sleeker and matching the quality you see on successful channels. As you gain design skills, tighten up your channel graphics and your video end screens. As your income grows, consider hiring a professional to help you level up your visual branding.

About Page

Schedule time on your editorial calendar, about one month in, to review your About page. Make sure it's still consistent with your goals. Add links for new projects or websites, if relevant. And if your target audience has shifted, update your About page so that it speaks to the right people.

Tags and Keyword Research

With experience, your SEO research will improve. You'll figure out which tags attract visitors. Review the tags you've used for your channel and verify they are still relevant to your videos. If a video is not getting views, try changing the tags using SEO best practices. We discussed SEO and keyword research in Chapter Six.

Consistent Message

Create content that's consistent with your message or topic, and then stick with it. When you divide your following by posting videos on a different topic, people stop watching and unsubscribe. You can stray a little — to test out certain styles, for example — but don't overdo it.

Niche down your content as soon as possible to make your channel consistent. Subscribers will stay with you and get more deeply connected with your channel.

Consistent Uploads

We can't emphasize this enough: you must release videos regularly. Consistently posting content is the number one thing you can do to maximize your channel growth.

You might be wondering, *While I'm optimizing my channel, should I ever delete old videos?*

If you're considering deleting or hiding videos from your channel, don't do it, no matter how cringe-worthy they are. It's best to save the delete option for the times when you make a bigger mistake or encounter a tech issue.

Three or four months into the process, you might look back and see that your channel has been all over the place. This can happen as you hone your voice and niche. Instead of deleting videos that no longer match your message, set them to private. This way the videos are still accessible if you want to make them publicly available again in the future.

But a word of caution: when you set a video to private mode, you lose the watch hours you've accumulated from that video. And if you lose too many watch hours, you can be demonetized. However, this is easily fixed by setting private videos to public again. When you do this, you regain any watch hours associated with that video.

Another word of caution: when you make a video private, check that it doesn't appear in any playlists on your channel. If you neglect to take it off a playlist, viewers see a "video unavailable" notice. This doesn't look professional. So keep private videos out of your playlists.

Stay Up-To-Date With YouTube's Changes

As you optimize and improve your channel, be aware of YouTube's existing policies as well as any changes. Read notices they send by email and stay up-to-date so that you can adapt quickly and easily.

It's typical for YouTube to enact some changes every year. Companies pivot, work within new laws, or discover things that aren't working for their platform. Expect changes — adjusting to new policies is part of the game.

Action Steps

1. Explore the Analytics page for your YouTube channel. Write down your subscriber and watch time goals, along with today's date and your current statistics.

2. Now analyze your data. How is your channel doing? Can you find reasons why some videos are more successful than others? What types of videos engage your audience? Write down your findings so that you can improve your channel.

3. Add "Review Analytics" to your editorial calendar once every week for the first 90 days of your channel, and after that, monthly.

12

CONCLUSION

There's no limit to what YouTube can do for you, whether it's building your brand, marketing your business, or connecting with a loyal fan base around your passion or hobby.

Slow and steady wins the race. Put most of your time into your content, check your analytics, and believe in your future success. When you follow the steps in this book, you CAN create a fulfilling and profitable career on YouTube.

We hope you enjoyed this book as much as we enjoyed writing it and that you take advantage of the opportunity presented by YouTube. At its heart, YouTube is about connections. And connections, in any business, are gold.

YouTube is a way to build your contact list and form a community of loyal fans who want to watch your videos and buy your offerings. When people follow you on YouTube, they become a part of your world. They feel connected. And the feeling is mutual!

So how will you use the connections you make on YouTube?

How can YouTube's enormous audience (1.8 billion users per month) benefit you and your brand?

How can you bring your passions to life on YouTube or provide marketing for your company?

We encourage you to use the Companion Workbook as a review for all stages of your YouTube development. It walks through the steps to set up your channel, create videos, launch your channel on social media, connect with other channels for success, and read your analytics.

You can download the workbook here: **uploaduniversity.com/book-bonus/**

The sky's the limit, and your success on YouTube is within reach. YouTube can provide you with income, brand and business growth, loyal fans, and a platform for sharing ideas and connections. Onwards and upwards to YouTube success — we are rooting for you!

If you enjoyed this book, check out the other titles in the Make Money From Home series at sallyannmiller.com/books

NOTES

5. Set up Your YouTube Account (Step Two)

1. https://support.google.com/youtube/answer/2972003?hl=en

6. Record Your First Three Videos (Step Three)

1. https://creatoracademy.youtube.com/page/lesson/thumbnails#yt-creators-strategies-1

ABOUT GINA HORKEY

Gina Horkey is a married millennial mama to two precocious kiddos from Minnesota.

In addition to PodcastProductionSchool.com, she's also the founder of several websites: HorkeyHandBook.com, UploadUniversity.com, KidsVsBikini.com and GinaHorkey.com.

Gina has specialized in helping everyday folks learn hard digital marketing skills to launch their own service-based businesses online, working from the comfort of their own home (or anywhere!) since 2014.

Her background includes making a living as a professional writer, an online business marketing consultant and a decade of experience in the financial services industry.

ABOUT LUCAS ATKINSON

Lucas is a father, fisherman and serial entrepreneur from Minneapolis, Minnesota.

In 2014, Lucas left an established career making over $100,000. He went on to create multiple revenue streams all from working at his kitchen table.

Lucas has a daughter who developed epilepsy when she was 2 1/2 years old. This motivated him to work from home and free up his daily schedule so that he could meet his daughter's needs.

Partnering with Gina (his youngest Sister) has been an exciting new chapter in his life. Lucas looks forward to inspiring others who are following their own dreams.

EXCERPT: MAKE MONEY AS A PODCAST PRODUCER

GINA HORKEY, MELANIE SCROGGINS & HAILEY THOMAS

What if you could make a living doing something you love without having anyone to answer to?

Imagine what life would be like if you had the freedom to set your own hours, work wherever you like, and choose the projects you work on.

You're here because you're hungry to do something different. You're ready to take control of your career and transform the way you work. Plus, you want to find out what this podcasting thing is all about.

Or maybe you're hearing about this virtual or remote work concept for the first time.

Your reasons may be as simple as wanting to ditch that hour-long commute each way to work. Or you need a career that lets you work from home while raising your kids. You dream about working in your yoga pants—and not having a bossy manager to report to.

Or perhaps you already have a few clients under your belt. You've dipped your toes into the entrepreneurial waters, and now you realize breaking into podcast production services might be perfect for you.

Maybe you picked up this book out of curiosity. You might always have a new podcast running through your headphones—but you never realized it was possible to learn how to establish your own podcasting career.

The good news: it's probably much easier to land a gig working on the podcast *Serial* than on the TV show *Stranger Things*!

Regardless of where you're at in your journey, we're here to help. At the end of the day, you want to make a living doing something you love, right?

If you stick with us, you'll learn a lot and finally realize your dream of building a business that fits around your life—not the other way around.

But you might be wondering who the authors are behind this book.

We're three ladies who came together to connect entrepreneurs with clients who need podcast support services. Our online course and brand, *Podcast Production School,* is designed to teach students the hard skills and strategies needed to launch, manage, and grow podcasts for small businesses.

It's our goal to teach you how to use the skills you already have to build a successful, sustainable, and flexible podcast production business supporting entrepreneurs from anywhere in the world.

The truth is we all take different paths to working online.

All three of us started in traditional nine-to-five jobs. We followed the traditional career path we were taught growing up. You go to college, find a job, and stick with that job for the rest of your life.

Sound familiar? Perhaps you heard a different message growing up. But that's the lesson we picked up in our homes.

It's how we found ourselves in the corporate world. Maybe you're in the same boat. You may have a full-time job that looks amazing on paper, yet you can't shake the feeling you were meant for more.

We've been there. And one day, we each finally realized that we weren't made for the nine-to-five life.

So we started to explore the possibilities. We discovered that building a flexible long-term business filled with serving clients you actually like isn't a pipe dream at all.

But it does come with its own set of challenges.

The Challenges of Freelancing

Since we began freelancing, we've had the opportunity to work with dozens of entrepreneurs and small business owners worldwide. However, our success didn't happen overnight. Launching a side hustle isn't exactly a walk in the park—there's no perfect formula.

And while hustling to build a business is a process of growth, the good news is that we're all in this together.

Of course, we each ran into unique challenges on the road to success. Yet, we ended up facing many of the same fears despite our different situations. If you're thinking of building a freelance podcasting business, you probably share the same concerns about forging your own path too.

You worry that you lack the technical know-how to run podcasts and you're not sure where to even start.

You're scared that you won't be able to pay your bills. You don't want to fail at building a business and end up going broke in the process.

You're afraid of rejection. How do you muster up the courage to pitch new clients? What if they think you don't have enough experience?

We know the feeling. Overcoming your fears can be the hardest part about becoming an entrepreneur. But here's the thing—if you don't feel afraid to pursue your dreams, they might not be big enough.

The healthy thing about fear is that a dose of reality can fuel your motivation and keep you moving in the right direction.

We dig deeper into those bumps in the road in the upcoming chapters of this book. And we share exactly what it took to overcome our doubts, get unstuck, and become a force to be reckoned with.

But before we get into that, you might be wondering...

Who the heck are 'we' and how did we all meet each other?!

Meet the Tantalizing Trio

Gina is the founder of HorkeyHandBook.com, a website aimed at helping others find or become freelance writers and/or virtual assistants. In 2014, Gina launched the website to showcase her own writing portfolio.

She ended up sharing her journey along the way as she built a successful writing-turned-virtual-assistant business. The website quickly morphed into education, training, and community for virtual assistants and freelance writers worldwide.

Since then, Gina's coached nearly 10,000 students and has helped hundreds upon hundreds of entrepreneurs find freelancers to support their businesses.

In 2017, Hailey completed Horkey HandBook's signature course, "30 Days or Less to Virtual Assistant Success." She quickly found success, landing clients left and right, and Gina talked her into sharing her success story on the blog.

Gina and Hailey continued to stay in touch and formed a friendship. Based on Hailey's success in her chosen niche of project management, Gina saw an opportunity and pitched Hailey on the idea of cocreating "Project Management for Virtual Assistants."

After all, learning new skills is highly needed in the marketplace today—no longer do you have to "go back to school" to learn them!

As Hailey continued to skyrocket her business growth, she decided to expand her marketing strategy and launched a podcast. That's when she hired Melanie as her Podcast Producer.

In fact, they met via a random Google search... how's that for fate?

Hailey and Melanie worked so well together that they teamed up to assist Hailey's clients with podcast production too. Their joint efforts servicing others' podcast production needs continued to thrive.

When Gina came to Hailey in the fall of 2019 with the idea of *Podcast Production School*, Hailey knew Melanie had to be a part of the team. After all, who else would be better to teach the tech side of podcasting to our students than a real-life producer?

Together with Gina's gift of teaching, Melanie's mad tech skills, and Hailey's obsession with all things organizational, *Podcast Production School* was born.

Naturally, we've also come together to write this book. We've been obsessed with the podcasting medium for years. The number of new shows is exploding. Which means there's an immense need for help behind the scenes.

And when we started, there weren't any complete resources on how to become a Podcast Producer. We had to learn on the fly. So we've written this book to save you the time and energy of having to figure it all out on your own.

Online business is such a small world and a beautifully collaborative space, right?

The 6 Steps to Making Money as a Podcast Producer

Let's talk about what it takes to earn a living supporting podcasters. The great news is the online business world is ripe with clients itching for help with one thing—podcasts!

In this book, we teach you all about the podcasting process. You'll learn how to confidently put yourself out there and conquer your fears around pitching new clients.

The basic steps to launching your podcast production business are:

1. Learn the tech skills.

2. Package your services.

3. Prospect for clients.

4. Start pitching.

5. Land your first podcast client.

6. Get paid!

These steps lay the foundation for everything you do moving forward. Once you take the first step, you'll begin to gather momentum and each action that follows becomes easier.

You can do this. No matter what your background. And we would be honored to support you on your journey. When we asked our students to share their thoughts, here's what a few had to say:

"I've been looking into working online for a long time, but I couldn't figure out what my "niche" should be. Just yesterday, I signed up my first podcast client from a lead in the community! I was never interested in starting a podcast of my own, so supporting other podcasts with the skills I have now is perfect for me."

"This course is great for the beginner or the virtual assistant that is looking to expand their services. It's great to have amazing support from Gina, Melanie, and Hailey; who are actively working in the industry!"

"I loved this information-packed course. I'm super excited to put the skills I learned to work in my business, and the best part is Gina, Mel, and Hailey will be there to help if I have questions and celebrate my wins with me. Love it!"

Podcast Producers come from all walks of life. Some of our students are entrepreneurs in the making, while others have been offering their freelance services for several years.

Will you be our next success story?

How to Transform Your Passion into Profit

We want you to be as successful as possible with this book.

That's why you'll find action steps to take as you make your way through the material. At the end of each chapter we've also provided you with checklists and worksheets to point you in the right direction.

For what it's worth, if you don't complete the steps or worksheets we provide you, then your odds of being successful aren't that great. Results come from action. It's not enough to passively consume the learning.

But if you follow these action steps and give it your all—we promise that you can master the skills needed to take over or help create a client's podcast, even if you're a total beginner. And we'll explain how to avoid the common roadblocks in the process.

In this book, we cover everything you need to know to transform your podcasting passion into a profitable freelance business.

Depending on how much time you have to devote to learning, you can lay the foundation for your podcast production business in the next 30 days or less.

By the time you get to the end, you should have a solid understanding of the steps you need to take and how to get started today!

Keep Reading Make Money As A Podcast Producer – available in online bookstores now!

Printed in Great Britain
by Amazon